Fun-filled Fascinating Facts and Untold Stories About Same-Sex Couples Throughout History:

Debunking Myths and Sharing Truths About Same-Sex Relationships, Even Between the Sheets.

NICCI BROCHARD
&
DR. BEN CHUBA

Fun-filled Fascinating Facts and Untold Stories About Same-Sex Couples Throughout History:

Debunking Myths and Sharing Truths About Same-Sex Relationships, Even Between the Sheets.

Book Formatting by: *Accuracy4sure*

Book cover design by: *Billy Design*

CROSSBORDER

New York, London, Quebec

Contents

Introduction

Picture this: Alexander the Great conquering the known world while texting his beloved Hephaestion sweet nothings (had smartphones existed in 336 BCE), or imagine Eleanor Roosevelt sliding into Lorena Hickok's DMs with the same passion she brought to championing human rights. History's greatest love stories didn't always follow the heteronormative script Hollywood keeps recycling, yet somehow these tales got buried deeper than Taylor Swift's old tweets.

Welcome to the ultimate historical tea-spilling session, where we're serving up centuries of same-sex romance with all the drama, passion, and occasional scandal that would make the Kardashians jealous. From ancient Greek symposiums that were basically the original Pride parties to Victorian "Boston marriages" that had more commitment than most modern celebrity unions, love has always found a way – even when society tried harder than a desperate influencer to suppress authentic expression.

Consider Leonardo da Vinci, who painted the Mona Lisa's enigmatic smile while nursing his own secret for his assistant Gian Giacomo Caprotti. Today, we'd call Leo the ultimate Renaissance polymath with impeccable taste in men, but back then, discretion was more crucial than choosing the right Instagram filter. Like Elton John before he became Sir Elton, these historical figures navigated love in the shadows while creating masterpieces that outlasted empires.

The ancient world was surprisingly progressive – think of it as the original "love is love" era. Sappho of Lesbos (yes, that Lesbos) was writing poetry about women that would make contemporary romance novels blush, while Roman Emperor Hadrian built an entire city to honor his deceased lover Antinous. These weren't casual flings; they were relationships with more staying power than most Hollywood marriages, complete with the kind of devotion that would inspire a dozen Nicholas Sparks novels.

Fast-forward through centuries of varying acceptance and persecution, and we find same-sex couples developing survival strategies that would impress any modern power couple. Take Gertrude Stein and Alice B. Toklas, who hosted the most exclusive salon in Paris while maintaining a partnership that lasted decades – essentially the early 20th century version of a power couple's joint Instagram account, but with Picasso and Hemingway as regular guests instead of lifestyle brands.

From the coded language of "confirmed bachelors" and "spinster friends" to the underground networks that rivaled any modern social media platform, LGBTQ+ individuals throughout history have demonstrated resilience, creativity, and an uncanny ability to find each other across time and geography. They've weathered everything from legal persecution to social ostracism, proving that love truly conquers all – even when "all" includes centuries of institutionalized discrimination.

These stories reveal universal truths about partnership: communication remains key (even when conducted through cryptic letters), compromise builds lasting relationships (especially when one partner is ruling an empire), and shared values matter more than public opinion (revolutionary concept, right?). Same-sex couples throughout history have mastered the art of creating chosen families, supporting each other's ambitions, and maintaining intimacy under pressure – lessons modern couples could apply regardless of orientation.

Get ready to meet history's most fascinating couples, whose love stories deserve the same recognition as any fairy tale, but with significantly better plot twists and considerably more authentic passion.

Enjoy the ride. Thank you in advance.

Ben and Nicci

Chapter 1

Adam and Steve –
Same-Sex Love at the Dawn of History

1. No Gays in Cave Days? Think again – even prehistoric pals likely paired off

Imagine a time when the height of fashion was a fur loincloth and "interior decorating" meant painting on cave walls. Some folks still insist that back in those days it was all strictly Adam-and-Eve, not Adam-and-Steve – as if our prehistoric ancestors were too busy discovering fire to discover each other. But spoiler alert: even in the *original* Stone Age community, there were probably a few Stone Age couples that would make the Flintstones look downright modern. In other words, same-sex love is no trendy new invention; it's older than the wheel, folks.

Picture two cavemen (let's call them Ugg and Ogg) returning from a mammoth hunt. They're not just high-fiving over a successful day's work; later, they're sharing a mammoth steak dinner by firelight, giving each other those *You complete me* looks across the campfire. Did their fellow cave dwellers bat an eye? Maybe, maybe not. They might have been too busy trying to survive saber-toothed tiger attacks to police who was snuggling with whom under the bearskin blankets. The truth is, the idea that "there were no gay cavepeople" holds about as much water as a woven-grass basket. Archaeological clues – from ambiguous cave art to same-gender burial arrangements – offer

4

tantalizing hints that sexual diversity is as ancient as humanity itself. Turns out *Brokeback Mountain* might have had a very, very early screening in some Paleolithic cave, minus the popcorn.

For example, one prehistoric cave carving in Italy seems to show two male figures in a rather intimate ritual. And over in remote China, the Kangjiashimenji rock carvings (~4,000 years old) depict an ancient lovefest complete with men pairing off with men and even gender-blurring characters dancing in the mix. In other words, our ancient ancestors were anything but straight-laced (pun intended). Essentially, these might be history's oldest illustrated same-sex rendezvous – literally carved in stone. If that doesn't debunk the "it never happened back then" myth, what will?

So the next time someone cracks that tired "Adam and Eve, not Adam and Steve" line, remind them that history strongly disagrees. Same-sex love is older than the wheel, period. Even cavemen likely needed cuddles and companionship. They might not have had a word for it, but they definitely had the feelings – love is love, be it in a damp cave or a high-rise condo. Marriage insight: Human nature doesn't really change. The heart wants what it wants, and it's wanted every possible configuration since time immemorial. If two Paleolithic pals could pair up under the stars and make it work, we modern folk with all our conveniences have zero excuse not to respect and embrace that love.

2. Epic of Gilgamesh: History's first bromance

Fast forward a few millennia to ancient Mesopotamia, where things are about to get epic – literally. The *Epic of Gilgamesh* is basically the blockbuster action-buddy-comedy of 2100 BCE, and at its heart is a relationship so profound that scholars still debate, "Were they or weren't they... you know?" Gilgamesh, the king of Uruk, starts off as a bit of a tyrannical meathead (imagine a superhero who hasn't discovered his moral compass yet – kind of like Thor before he learned humility). The gods, tired of his antics, decide to send him an equal: Enkidu, a wild man from the wilderness, custom-built to be Gilgamesh's best bud.

When Gilgamesh and Enkidu finally meet, it's the stuff of legend. They wrestle in the streets of Uruk – an ancient Mesopotamian meet-cute if ever there was one – and after a fierce contest of strength, something remarkable happens: the two men basically fall into an intense bromance on the spot. One translation even notes that they kissed each other and became companions. Yes, you read that right – kisses and hugs all around. If that doesn't blur the line between "no-homo bro hug" and "actually, kinda homo," I don't know what does. Gilgamesh's mom, the goddess Ninsun, certainly picked up on the vibe. Legend has it he dreamed about a meteor (or was it an axe?) that he embraced like a wife, and Mama Ninsun interpreted this as a sign that a man would come into his life whom he'd love like a wife. Cue Enkidu's entrance. (When your *mother* basically predicts your soulmate bromance, you know this is no ordinary friendship.)

From that point on, Gilgamesh and Enkidu are inseparable – slaying monsters by day, having deep heart-to-hearts by night. They journey to defeat the demon Humbaba together (think of it as a deadly camping trip with your ride-or-die partner). They even take on the Bull of Heaven as a duo. Through it all, they hold each other up, literally and emotionally. When Enkidu eventually falls ill and dies, Gilgamesh is shattered. He "weeps for Enkidu... bitterly like a mourning woman," as the epic describes. The mighty king is so grief-stricken that he abandons his palace to wander the wilderness, desperately seeking a way to bring his dear friend back or at least achieve immortality himself – anything to dull the pain of loss. If that's not love (whatever label you give it), it's at least devotion on a level that would make Shakespeare's characters jealous.

Call it a profound friendship or history's first same-sex love story – either way, their bond was extraordinary. Marriage insight: Whether your partner is your spouse or your best friend (or both), the best relationships make you a better person. Gilgamesh started as a tyrant and became a hero, all thanks to Enkidu. Sometimes the person who completes you shows up in the unlikeliest form (maybe not a wild hairy dude from the woods, but hey, everyone's type is different). The key is that when you find that person, you hold on and grow together. Find someone who can match your strength, calm your storms, and share your adventures (ideally with fewer monster battles) – that's a partnership worth going epic for.

3. Tomb of Two Gentlemen: An Egyptian tale of Niankhkhnum and Khnumhotep – two male royal manicurists buried in a loving embrace

Let's leave the Mesopotamian bromance and head to the land of pyramids and pharaohs, where we find perhaps the most Pinterest-worthy ancient couple ever: Niankhkhnum and Khnumhotep. These two gentlemen lived in Egypt about 4,400 years ago and shared a title that, to modern ears, sounds almost too on-the-nose – they were Overseers of the Royal Manicurists in the Palace of Pharaoh. Yes, ancient Egypt's royal nail technicians. (File this under: "Job titles that had to come with fabulous gossip.") By all accounts, Niankhkhnum and Khnumhotep were *work spouses* who very likely became real spouses in all but name, and they took the concept of "till death do us part" so seriously that even death was like, "Well, okay, you two can stick together."

How serious were they? In 1964, archaeologists discovered their joint tomb at Saqqara, and the walls tell a beautiful story. The tomb paintings show the two men embracing, holding hands, and touching noses – the most intimate pose allowed in Egyptian art (basically the equivalent of a kiss). In one scene they stand nose-to-nose as lovingly as any husband and wife in other tombs. They're even described in inscriptions as "royal confidants," and their names are inscribed together as a pair. It's like the hieroglyphs are literally saying "these two belong together." Couple goals, Old Kingdom edition!

Now, for the skeptics: yes, both men had wives and children (plot twist!). But the way they're depicted together in the tomb has led many Egyptologists to conclude that Niankhkhnum and Khnumhotep were more than just colleagues or buddies. For one, in the tomb art, Khnumhotep occupies the position usually reserved for a wife, and Niankhkhnum's wife was even chiseled out of one scene. Talk about making a statement in stone! It's the ancient equivalent of Photoshopping your spouse out of the family picture – *savage*, Niankhkhnum. Clearly, the relationship that mattered most to these two was *theirs*.

Notably, we've found no papyrus whispering scandal about their relationship. It seems this arrangement wasn't viewed as some huge shock – possibly it was even respected or simply accepted. They lived their lives, did their royal manicures, had families (life is complicated, even in 2400 BCE), but ultimately chose to be buried together, side by side, as if to say *this* was the partnership that truly mattered. Marriage insight: True love finds a way – even if you have to carve it in hieroglyphs. A strong relationship is built on everyday companionship and trust. Niankhkhnum and Khnumhotep worked together, dined together, were literally entombed together. If that's not sticking it out through thick and thin (and afterlife), what is? And hey, maybe the secret to lasting love is occasionally giving your partner a manicure. It certainly worked for these two!

4. Gods (and Goddesses) Behaving Badly: Queer mythology 101 – from Zeus and his boy-toy Ganymede to gender-bending deities

If you thought mortal history had all the fun, wait until you hear what the gods were up to. Spoiler: it's a hot mess of queer shenanigans up on Mount Olympus (and in pretty much every other pantheon) that would make a modern soap opera writer blush. The ancients didn't just have LGBTQ+ humans – they projected every flavor of love and lust onto their deities, too.

Let's start with the head honcho of the Greek gods, Zeus – a deity with a well-documented *enthusiasm* for, well, everyone. Zeus, king of the gods, had an extremely open mind in love. He even fell for a gorgeous Trojan prince, Ganymede – whisking him up to Olympus to be his cupbearer (and lover). Hera was livid, but even she couldn't stop Zeus. If the chief god could have a boyfriend, the ancients clearly weren't too worried about same-sex shenanigans. (Moral of the story: when even Zeus is saying "love is love," it's hard to argue it's against the natural order!)

Now, hop over to other cultures: you'll find queer themes tucked in mythologies everywhere. In Hindu lore, the gods sometimes literally switch gender as part of their divine pastimes. Case in point: Vishnu, a male deity, once transformed into the irresistibly beautiful female form of Mohini – so enchanting that Shiva (yes, *the* mighty Shiva) fell head over heels in love with *him/her*. They didn't just flirt, either; depending on the version of the myth, they got very cozy (and even parented a divine child). No one in the story bats an eye at this divine same-sex attraction – it's just gods being gods. The message from the ancient storytellers is loud and clear: gender? Optional. Love and desire? Boundless, even for the gods.

So, what do we learn from these divine antics? Simply that love and desire have always been part of the natural (and supernatural) order. Next time someone claims queerness is "unnatural," point them to Zeus or Vishnu and tell them to take it up with the gods. Marriage insight: The myths remind us that there's no one "right" way to love. Ancient deities shaped their forms and companions to suit their fancy – a cosmic endorsement of being true to oneself. For us mortals, the takeaway is that a healthy relationship doesn't have to fit a narrow mold. Love is versatile and ever-present, so embrace what feels authentic to you (just maybe practice a bit more honesty and fidelity than Zeus did – it'll save everyone some heartache).

5. Ancient Sex Ed: The Kama Sutra's guide to gay love

By now it's clear that same-sex love isn't some modern trend. But if you need written proof that our ancestors not only acknowledged it but even included it in their how-to manuals, look no further than ancient India's Kama Sutra. Yes, *that* Kama Sutra – the one known for its acrobatic lovemaking positions and cheeky advice on romance. Compiled around the 4th century CE by the sage Vatsyayana, the Kama Sutra is actually a guide to living one's best life (pleasure is just one part of it), and believe it or not, it devotes an entire chapter to same-sex intimacy between men. In a text written over 1,600 years ago, it straight-up says that homosexual acts "are to be engaged in and enjoyed for their own sake as one of the arts". In other words, two dudes being together isn't some aberration – it's an art form, a source of joy, something to be pursued because it's pleasurable and fulfilling, end of story.

To put this in perspective: while later prudish empires were clutching their pearls and pretending that only one-man-one-woman was "natural," the Kama Sutra was essentially saying, "Hey, if it feels good for both of you, go for it." It provides detailed descriptions of male-male erotic techniques (yes, including the *ahem* oral variety) without batting an eye. It even categorizes men who desire other men as a "third nature," acknowledging that for some people this is just how they are – a pretty astute recognition of diversity for an era that long ago. Basically, a Sanskrit scholar in antiquity was more open-minded about gay sex than a lot of Victorian gentlemen (or certain modern politicians).

To top it off, ancient Indian art even immortalized this openness in stone. The medieval temples of Khajuraho are famously covered in erotic sculptures depicting every conceivable combination of lovemaking – and that includes a few discreet but clear depictions of men enjoying each other's company (with onlookers, no less, because apparently ancient threesomes were a thing). They clearly weren't shy about these matters.

Erotic sculpture from Khajuraho temple (10th century CE) depicting two males in an intimate pose. Ancient Indian art and texts like the Kama Sutra openly acknowledged same-sex love and desire as a natural part of life.

Now, this isn't to say ancient India was some eternal queer utopia – times changed, and later on, colonial prudery cast a long shadow. But the Kama Sutra stands as undeniable evidence that long before modern debates, there was an era in India that treated same-sex love as just another beautiful part of life. Its authors faced the topic head-on, basically saying, "If it's consensual and fun, here's how to make it *really* fun. Enjoy, and namaste."

Marriage insight: Intimacy and love thrive on openness and communication. The ancients understood that pleasure and connection are natural art forms in a relationship. If a 1,600-year-old guide could encourage people to be honest and playful about their desires, surely we can too. Sometimes the secret to lasting passion is simply being willing to learn (and try) something new together. After all, our ancestors weren't shy – so why should we be?

Thanks! I'll now draft a full 3,000-word version of Chapter 2 — 'Achilles' "Best Friend" – Queer Love in Classical Greece' — written in a humorous, witty, and conversational tone, formatted like a book manuscript with clear section headers and flowing transitions. I'll deliver it here in parts for smoother reading.

Chapter 2

Achilles' "Best Friend" –
Queer Love in Classical Greece

They were just very good friends. – Every history teacher ever, winking about Achilles and Patroclus (or insert any number of same-sex duos from antiquity). Welcome to Classical Greece, where "best friend" often meant *soulmate* and love wasn't confined by gender roles or modern labels. In this chapter, we're pulling back the curtain (or rather, the toga) on some of the most fabulous same-sex relationships in Greek lore and life. From poetesses serenading their girlfriends on Lesbos to an entire army of boyfriends who literally fought side by side, get ready for some ancient romance that's as epic as a Homeric simile – and way more fun.

Sappho's Island of Lesbos – Poetry and passion among women

Ancient fresco of a woman with a stylus (often identified as Sappho) from Pompeii, reflecting the poetess's literary side. Sappho of Lesbos was basically the OG lesbian icon – and we mean that literally. Living around 600 BC on the island of Lesbos, she ran with a circle of ladies who were writing poetry, singing songs, and crushing on each other long before it was cool. In a world where women were mostly supposed to weave and bear kids, Sappho was strumming the lyre and dropping verses about the fiery passion she felt for her female friends.

13

Think of her as the Taylor Swift of the archaic age, if Taylor wrote exclusively about her girlfriends and none of her boyfriends. Sappho's poems were so famous for their sapphic (yes, named after her) flavor that the very name of her home, Lesbos, gave us the term "lesbian." Talk about leaving your mark!

She wasn't shy about it either – her lyrics speak directly of longing and love for women. One fragment describes her heart beating fast at the sight of a favorite gal pal, tongue tied, sweat pouring – basically the 6th-century BC version of catching feelings hard. Sappho ran what might have been a sort of creative girls' club (a poetry school or just a really happening salon on Lesbos) where upper-class women bonded over music, verse, and probably the ancient equivalent of truth-or-dare. Unsurprisingly, later generations alternated between celebrating her and clutching their pearls. (Even Plato, the philosopher, reportedly called her the "Tenth Muse" – she was that revered. Move over Calliope, Sappho's in town!).

Ancient comedians, uncomfortable with her popularity and obvious affection for women, tried to straight-wash her story. They jokingly invented a husband for Sappho named Kerkylas of Andros – which, get this, roughly translates to "Dick from Man Island." Yes, really. That's like saying "Oh sure, she's totally straight, she married *Mr. Phallus McManly*." Nice try, ancient trolls. Another myth claimed Sappho leapt off a cliff over a male lover (the ferryman Phaon). But let's be real: that tale reads like ancient fan-fiction to satisfy those who couldn't handle a woman who wasn't pining for a dude. The truth is Sappho didn't need a tragic male love story – she was too busy being the queen bee of lesbian love poetry.

Marriage lesson with flair: In Sappho's world, love was love, and she didn't apologize for it. She teaches us that pouring your heart out in a poem or song for your beloved is timeless seduction – way classier than a late-night "u up?" text. Also, when society tells you to fit in a mold, break it and rhyme about it. If your devotion can coin new vocabulary (hello "sapphic" love), you know you're doing something right in the romance department!

My Big Fat Greek Man-crush – From Achilles and Patroclus to Zeus's affairs

A scene of Achilles tending Patroclus's wounds on an ancient Greek vase – a tender "bromance" moment that had more going on beneath the surface. When it comes to male-male love, ancient Greece was basically the land of the epic man-crush. Case in point: Achilles and Patroclus, the dynamic duo of Homer's *Iliad*. These two were tighter than spandex on a Spartan – inseparable on and off the battlefield. Sure, some textbooks coyly call Patroclus "Achilles' best friend," but honey, the *feels* in that story say otherwise. Achilles was the mightiest warrior among the Greeks, but his true weak spot wasn't his famous heel; it was his love for Patroclus. When Patroclus dies in the war (uh, spoiler alert for a 3,000-year-old story?), Achilles completely loses his cool – we're talking ugly crying, refusal to eat, man-slaughtering rampages, the whole package. If that's not true love, Plato can have my Netflix password.

Ancient audiences certainly interpreted Achilles and Patroclus as more than pals. In fact, Greeks in later centuries held them up as the ultimate example of warrior-lovers. They even squabbled over who was the "lover" and who the "beloved" (the ancient equivalent of debating who's the Michelle and who's the Beyoncé in the relationship). Regardless, their bond was legendary. Modern pop culture has tiptoed around it – the 2004 *Troy* film awkwardly called Patroclus Achilles' *cousin* (oh come on, nobody buys that – we all saw those lingering looks, Brad Pitt!). Thankfully, recent retellings like Madeline Miller's novel *The Song of Achilles* go full heart-eyes emoji on their love story. Bottom line: Achilles + Patroclus = Greek antiquity's hottest power couple (move over, Zeus and Hera – these two actually liked each other).

Now, speaking of Zeus… the king of the gods had his own same-sex escapade, and it's one for the tabloids. Zeus was notorious for his *hetero* affairs (the man has a whole Bestiary of Shame – swan, bull, golden rain, you name it). But he also fancied a pretty boy: Ganymede, a Trojan prince so gorgeous that Zeus said "I gotta have him" and literally kidnapped him in the form of a giant eagle. (Consent? Never heard of it, apparently.) Ganymede ends up as Zeus's personal cupbearer on Mount Olympus – which is just a divine euphemism for "boyfriend in residence." Hera, Zeus's long-suffering wife, was unsurprisingly not amused, but at least this fling didn't produce any demigod bastards to clutter the family reunions. The Greeks embraced the tale – to them, if Zeus could have a male lover, why not mere mortals? They immortalized Ganymede as the Aquarius constellation and even named one of Jupiter's moons after him much later. Zeus and Ganymede basically set the precedent: male-male love was not only natural, it was downright heavenly (though, note to humans: don't imitate the eagle abduction part). Other gods followed suit: Apollo had his beloved Hyacinthus (ending in tragedy *and* a flower – extra drama), and even Hercules had a male companion, Iolaus, who was so adored that Greek couples would worship at his tomb, hoping for a love as epic. When love between men is literally myth-endorsed and star-sanctioned, you know the culture was here for it.

Marriage lesson: Don't let pride or outside opinion closet your affection – Achilles could have used a good couples therapist before things got out of hand. And absolutely do not follow Zeus's dating strategies (no undercover swan seductions or eagle carry-offs, please). Instead, raise a toast (like at those old symposium parties) to honesty in love. If he doesn't mourn you with world-altering fury like Achilles did for Patroclus, or move the stars for you like Zeus did for Ganymede, maybe up your standards! Love, Greek style, demands nothing less.

The Sacred Band – An army of 150 lover pairs in Thebes who fought (and snuggled) side by side

The Lion of Chaeronea memorial, erected to honor the Sacred Band of Thebes – because nothing says "love conquers all" like a giant stone kitty guarding your mass grave. Now, if you thought Achilles and Patroclus were #CoupleGoals, wait till you hear about the Sacred Band of Thebes. This wasn't just one pair of lovebirds – it was 150 male couples, hand-picked to form an elite fighting unit. Yes, you read that right: Thebes' secret weapon was basically a 300-man cuddle puddle with spears. Their logic? Warriors would fight like demons to impress and protect their lovers at their side. (Aww, and also yikes.) The Sacred Band was founded in the 4th century BC and soon became the ancient world's answer to the Navy SEALs – if every SEAL had a battle boyfriend. They trained together, lived together, probably argued over whose turn it was to polish the armor – and they absolutely wrecked their enemies on the battlefield. In one famous victory at Leuctra (371 BC), these love-warriors helped smash Sparta's army, ending Spartan military dominance. Talk about the power of love (cue Huey Lewis music) – Thebes literally weaponized romance and it worked!

The Sacred Band's existence blows a hole in the notion that love makes warriors "soft." Quite the opposite – it made them fearless. Each pair consisted of an older partner (the erastes) and a younger partner (eromenos), bound by sacred oaths (they even pledged their love at the shrine of Iolaus – Hercules's male lover – essentially an ancient same-sex wedding ceremony before deployment). How's that for commitment? They ate, slept, and drilled together; you can bet they knew each other's strengths and flaws intimately (in every sense). Sure, it might have gotten awkward if a couple had a lovers' spat – picture two spearmen giving each other the silent treatment in phalanx formation – but on the whole, love was their strength. In battle, they were said to be utterly unflinching, each man determined not to disgrace himself in front of his beloved. Imagine fighting with 150 dearly beloveds watching your back; you'd be heroic too or die trying.

Die they eventually did – heroically. In 338 BC, at the Battle of Chaeronea, the Sacred Band met their end against Philip II of Macedon and his son, a teenaged Alexander (yes, *that* Alexander – we'll get to him next). Surrounded and refusing to yield, they were slain to the last man. When the dust settled, the Macedonian king (not known for mushiness) was reportedly so moved by their valor and loyalty that he ordered a memorial erected: that big stone lion still stands in Chaeronea today, guarding the mass grave of 254 fallen lovers. Talk about poignant – even the enemies paid tribute. Philip allegedly said, "Woe to the people who think these men did anything shameful" upon learning they were all couples. In other words, *respect*. It took modern armies until the 21st century to say "hey, maybe gay folks can fight," but ancient Thebes figured it out in a hot minute.

Marriage lesson: The Sacred Band teaches us that a couple who trusts each other can take on the world – or at least 4th-century BC battlefields. Having your soulmate as your battle buddy? Unbeatable. (Just maybe leave the literal sword-fighting out of modern marital disputes.) Teamwork, trust, and mutual devotion turn out to be the ultimate secret weapons, whether you're defeating Spartans or just conquering life's daily challenges with your partner by your side.

Alexander the Great's Great Love – The conqueror's soulmate Hephaestion

Alexander the Great conquered half the known world, but he also had a tender side-arm: his lifelong companion Hephaestion. These two Macedonian bros were inseparable from boyhood, and not in a "no-homo" way – more like a "we share one soul in two bodies" way (actual vibe per ancient sources). Alexander himself encouraged the comparison to Achilles and Patroclus. When they visited the ruins of Troy, Alexander laid a wreath on Achilles' tomb and *Hephaestion* laid one on Patroclus', making a bold statement of "yup, that's us." The ancient historian Aelian even notes this, basically outing Hephaestion as Alexander's Patroclus (ancient subtweeting at its finest). And the Persian royalty could tell something was up: there's a story that Darius's mother, meeting Alexander's inner circle, mistook the tall, handsome Hephaestion for Alexander and apologized. Alexander quipped, "No apologies needed, he too is Alexander." Talk about *couple goals* – Alexander straight-up said "he is my other self." You can almost hear the collective aww (and faint gasps) in the royal court.

On campaign, Hephaestion was Alexander's right-hand man (and likely the one warming Alexander's tent at night). Sure, Alexander had wives – a king's gotta secure those alliances – but none of them got the love and devotion he showed Hephaestion. In fact, when one of Alexander's new Persian brides supposedly complained about her husband spending more time with Hephaestion than with her, it was kind of an open secret. Sadly, their story, like most in antiquity, veered into tragedy. In 324 BC, Hephaestion suddenly fell ill and died (possibly of fever or some nasty poisoning – ancient historians differ, but not on Alexander's reaction). And *boy* did Alexander lose it. He wept for days, refused food, cut his hair (an homage to Achilles mourning Patroclus), and according to some sources, had the poor doctor executed for failing to save his beloved (extreme, much?). He ordered a massive funeral pyre built in Babylon and staged an epic send-off for Hephaestion that made Princess Diana's funeral look like a backyard BBQ. He even petitioned the gods to grant Hephaestion divine honors. Basically, Alexander went full "I can't live without you" – and indeed, he died himself just eight months later. Coincidence? The romantics would say his heart was broken beyond repair.

Their bond was so legendary that even in a macho, conquest-driven culture, people respected it. No snickering behind the king's back (would *you* snicker at a guy who can defeat entire armies?). Instead, Alexander's men saw Hephaestion as *almost* king by association – and Alexander trusted him with that status. They were truly antiquity's power couple: ruling, strategizing, and yes, likely canoodling across continents. It's fitting that in modern times, many see them as one of history's great love stories, period. Where others had a bromance, Alexander and Hephaestion had a full-on "bromance" (emphasis on romance).

Marriage lesson: Find yourself a partner who doubles as your BFF, confidant, and ride-or-die. Treat them like another you (Alexander literally did). And if fate separates you, honor their memory in whatever grand way feels right (though maybe skip the whole executing the doctor step). Alexander's life shows that conquering the world means nothing if you don't have your soulmate to share it. True love might not *literally* burn up a $10 million funeral pyre for you, but hey, it's nice to know someone might want to.

Fact vs. Fiction – Debunking the idea that Greeks only had pederasty

It's time to bust the biggest myth: "Ancient Greek same-sex relationships were just older men preying on young boys." *Wrong-o!* Sure, the Greeks had a custom of pederasty – an older mentor bonding (yes, sometimes physically) with a youth – which modern folks rightfully side-eye. But that was only one slice of the rainbow pie. As we've seen, Greek love came in all varieties. There were lifelong male-male partnerships between peers (hi there, Sacred Band and Alexander & Hephaestion), not just May-December flings. There were passionate female-female relationships (Sappho and her gal pals sending love poems like it's Ancient Greek Snapchat). And those mentor-youth romances? In ideal form, they were supposed to evolve into lasting friendships once the youngster grew up – sometimes they evolved into lifelong love affairs too. The Greeks didn't even have the concept of "sexual orientation" like us; they just assumed people could find beauty in any gender under the right circumstances. In other words, they didn't box people in as "straight or gay" – they were too busy philosophizing about whether love makes you a better citizen (it was basically their version of a TED Talk topic).

Ancient Greek society actually celebrated same-sex love in many ways. Cities like Thebes literally built a military around it. Athens erected statues of Harmodius and Aristogeiton, a pair of lover-heroes who assassinated a tyrant – they were hailed as the founders of Athenian democracy. (Imagine, the birth of democracy attributed to a gay couple with knives – you can't make this stuff up!). Poets like Sappho and playwrights like Aristophanes wrote about same-sex desire openly. At drinking parties, an older dude might lift a cup and toast to the handsome young man he fancied, and nobody would spit out their wine. Yes, there were also crude jokes and some moralists clucking about "excess" – every era has its haters – but on the whole, the Greeks were pretty chill by comparison to later historical periods. The real fiction here is the notion that the ancient world didn't recognize true same-sex love. Tell that to Achilles, who literally caused and ended a war over his man. Tell that to Alexander, who called his boyfriend another himself. Tell it to the Sacred Band, who went down together in a blaze of glory rather than be separated. These aren't one-off exceptions; they're part of a broad pattern: the Greeks knew love is love, in many forms.

By the time the prudish Romans and later Victorian scholars got around to writing about Greek habits, they over-focused on the salacious bits (because of course they did). Thus we got this skewed idea of "dirty old Greeks and their boy toys." But that's like describing an elephant by its tail – ridiculously incomplete. In reality, ancient Greek relationships ranged from the profoundly spiritual to the intensely carnal, between men and women, women and women, men and men, older and younger, and everything in between. The common thread? Human connection and love, with all the messiness and magic that entails. So the next time someone claims gay love is a modern trend or a sinful phase, remind them that a bunch of toga-wearing, chariot-racing pagans were forming deep same-sex bonds thousands of years ago – sometimes for a season, sometimes for life, often celebrated, sometimes complicated, but undeniably *there*. History has receipts! In truth, the Greeks prove that love – queer love included – is as old as humanity and just as enduring. Or as a Greek might put it: Eros (love) has many faces, darling, and all of them have been around forever.

Chapter 3

When in Rome... Do as the Romans (Which Was *A Lot*)

Caesar's Everywoman & Everyman Reputation

Julius Caesar was many things—general, statesman, fashion trendsetter in a laurel wreath—but "prude" was not on the list. In fact, he garnered a reputation that would make even modern gossip columnists blush. This was a man jokingly called "every woman's husband and every man's wife" by his contemporaries, and they weren't just being poetic. Rumors swirled in Rome's forums that Caesar didn't discriminate when it came to romance. If hearts had status updates back then, Caesar's might have read: "It's complicated (with everyone)."

So, about that scandalous nickname: the story goes that Caesar, in his younger days, had a *special* friendship with King Nicomedes of Bithynia. "Friendship" might be putting it lightly—whispers around the Roman water cooler (er, aqueduct) hinted that the young Roman emissary and the Bithynian king were cuddling up like a power couple. One rumor quipped that Nicomedes "made an honest man" of Caesar, implying our would-be emperor was playing the blushing bride in that international fling. *Scandalous*, right? It's the kind of juicy gossip that would have had TMZ scrambling. Imagine the headlines if a rising political star today shacked up with a foreign king—Twitter would implode and late-night comedians would have a field day. Well, ancient Rome didn't have Twitter, but it had gossip—and boy, did that gossip stick.

Caesar's rivals certainly weren't above milking this story for all it was worth. Political smear campaigns are a timeless sport, after all. Cicero, Rome's resident silver-tongued gossip, loved to drop innuendos about the Bithynian escapade whenever he could. And when Caesar celebrated a triumph (a grand victory parade) for conquering Gaul, guess what his own soldiers cheekily chanted as his chariot rolled by? "Caesar conquered Gaul, but Nicomedes conquered Caesar." Ouch. Not the soundtrack you want for your victory lap, but there it was – his troops playfully roasting him in verse while the crowds cheered. Picture Caesar trying to look dignified on his chariot, all while his legionnaires are marching behind him singing a saucy rhyme about his royal liaison. Multitasking, Roman-style: conquering nations by day, dodging shade by night.

Yet, for all the snickers and side-eye, Caesar's everywoman/everyman reputation didn't stop him from climbing the ladder to ultimate power. Rome cared more about his battlefield conquests than his bedroom rumors. If anything, the titillating gossip just added to his legend. Some Romans were in awe ("Did you hear? He even seduced a *king*! What a player!"), while others were aghast ("No real man would play the *wife!*", huffed the conservative types, clutching their pearls – or whatever the ancient equivalent was). Through it all, Caesar played it cool. He never publicly confirmed or denied the Nicomedes story – a classic power move, keeping everyone guessing. Instead, he doubled down on his macho image: wooing countless women, bedding noblewives, even fathering a child with Cleopatra. He basically said, "Think I was Nicomedes's *wife*? Fine.

Then I'll be every woman's husband, too." Julius wasn't about to let one scandal define him. Thus, the legend of Julius "every woman's husband, every man's wife" was cemented for eternity.

What's the takeaway from Caesar's capers? Perhaps it's that power and charisma can get you away with a lot. Enemies will gossip and soldiers might sing bawdy ballads about you, but if you're successful enough, it all just becomes part of your mystique. Maybe the little marriage lesson here is this: don't do anything with a king that you wouldn't want sung about in your victory parade. In other words, personal antics have a way of going public – even in 45 BCE. More broadly, gossip didn't stop Caesar; if anything, it fueled his fame. Love (or lust) finds a way to write its own legend. Caesar marched on, unfazed, proving that sometimes *all* press is good press when you're destined to wear a laurel crown.

Hadrian and Antinous

If Julius Caesar's love life was a juicy tabloid, Emperor Hadrian's love story with Antinous is more of an epic romance novel—complete with a heart-wrenching ending. Let's set the scene: Hadrian, ruling the Roman Empire in the 2nd century, is powerful, cultured, and probably a little bored with the usual courtly duties. Then along comes Antinous, a Greek teenager with the face of a marble statue (ironically, he'd eventually *become* a bunch of marble statues, but we'll get to that). Antinous is youthful and radiant; think of him as the ultimate trophy boyfriend – except with genuine love involved, not just arm candy. Hadrian was so smitten that he basically took the kid on a never-ending road trip around the empire. When the emperor is your sugar daddy, you tour the world in imperial style.

Their bond became the talk of the imperial inner circle. Sure, Hadrian had a wife (Empress Sabina), but his heart belonged to Antinous in a way that made ancient historians raise their eyebrows and later gossipers swoon. This was no casual fling. Hadrian and Antinous were inseparable – hunting together, visiting Egyptian pyramids together – doing all the cute couple things, imperial-style. It was as close to a public same-sex love affair as you could get when you also happened to *be the law*. Hadrian wasn't shouting it from the rooftops, but he wasn't hiding his affection either. Imagine a modern leader bringing a "special advisor" on every state trip and gazing fondly at him during speeches – people would notice, right? Well, people noticed Hadrian and Antinous.

Then comes the heartbreak worthy of a Netflix season finale: in 130 AD, Antinous drowned in the Nile under mysterious circumstances. Nobody knows if it was an accident, suicide, or something stranger, but the point is — Antinous was gone, and Hadrian was absolutely devastated. When an emperor is heartbroken, he doesn't just cry into a pillow. Hadrian went full-on extra in his grief. First, he declares Antinous a god. Yes, *a literal deity*. One minute Antinous is a commoner with great hair, the next he's officially deified as the god of… well, mostly of Hadrian's affections (okay, they said "youth and fertility," but we know what was driving this). Talk about raising your boyfriend's status!

But wait, there's more. Hadrian even founded a city in Egypt at the spot where Antinous died, naming it Antinoopolis — basically a giant "In Memory of My Love" billboard on the map of the world. He commissioned countless statues of Antinous, spread them across the empire, and established temples where his new deity could be worshipped. Soon Antinous's face was everywhere; the 19-year-old pretty boy became a sensation, literally idolized. Subtle, Hadrian was not. Antinous achieved in death the kind of fame most people could only dream of. The emperor made sure of that.

From a modern point of view, this whole saga gives us serious "grand romantic gesture" goals — albeit completely unrealistic ones for us non-emperors. Most of us might name a star or donate a park bench in memory of a loved one; Hadrian made his lover a god. Normal scales of romance just didn't apply here. Under all that imperial pomp, though, Hadrian's devotion was almost disarmingly sincere. He didn't care if traditionalists side-eyed him like, "Deifying pretty boys now, are we?" The way Hadrian saw it, Antinous deserved to live forever – and being emperor, he had the means to make sure he sort of did.

What marriage or relationship lesson can we draw from Hadrian and Antinous? Perhaps it's that when you truly love someone, you want to immortalize them (though maybe stick to naming a star or getting a tattoo, rather than building entire cities and religions in their honor). Hadrian basically invented the ultimate PDA: Public Deification of Affection. His extra-mile devotion sets an awfully high bar for the rest of us. But it reminds us that even the most powerful people are, at the end of the day, driven by matters of the heart. Love can make emperors act like besotted fools – just on a scale that includes marble statues and city-wide memorials.

Nero's Big Fat Gay Weddings

We now turn to Emperor Nero, proof that the word "dysfunctional" always has room to push the envelope. If Hadrian's love was a touching romance, Nero's was an over-the-top reality show. This infamous emperor didn't just "fiddle" while Rome burned – he was also fiddling with the very definition of marriage, in ways that left Romans equal parts scandalized and confused.

Let's break down Nero's matrimonial misadventures. First up: a young boy named Sporus. Nero spotted this teen and disturbingly noted the boy's resemblance to his recently deceased wife, Poppaea. Now, most grieving husbands might commission a nice portrait or pen a poem to mourn their late wife. Nero's approach? Castrate the boy and marry him as his new wife. You read that correctly. He effectively said, "Honey, I can't bring my darling Poppaea back, so you'll have to do – after a little surgery." Talk about skipping a few steps in the dating process! Nero even had Sporus dressed up like an Empress – lavish robes, jewelry, veil and all – and paraded him around in public as his bride. If there were tabloids then, the wedding photo would've been on every front page: Emperor Nero with his blushing boy-bride. It's like Nero watched *My Fair Lady* and decided to remake it as a twisted Roman reboot (minus any consent from poor Sporus).

Believe it or not, Nero wasn't done. A while later, perhaps deciding he also wanted to see how the other side of the altar lived, Nero married a freedman named Pythagoras. (Not the triangle guy – a different Pythagoras, though Nero's love life did have all sorts of strange angles.) This time, Nero played the bride. He donned a bridal veil, complete with the wedding dress, and solemnly wed Pythagoras in a full ceremony, with Nero taking the role of the "wife." Yes, the emperor of Rome walked himself down the aisle. You can imagine the reaction in the imperial court: jaws on the floor, eyes popping, perhaps a few nervous giggles quickly stifled because who's going to laugh openly at the emperor in a wedding gown? Nero basically said, "Gender roles? Never heard of 'em." He was an equal-opportunity spouse: first the groom in one wedding, then the bride in another. RuPaul would be proud – Nero was serving gender-fluid realness in 64 AD like nobody's business.

If you think the Romans around him might have paused and said, "Uh, Your Highness… what are we doing?", you'd be right. Even in freewheeling ancient Rome, this was eyebrow-raising. Sure, Romans were used to emperors doing wacky stuff, but public same-sex weddings with the emperor switching roles? That was premium gossip fodder. Historians like Tacitus and Suetonius report these events with a mix of outrage and titillation, as if they themselves can't quite believe what they're writing. The imperial court must have been half terrified of Nero and half morbidly fascinated – like watching a tiger on a leash, wondering what crazy thing would happen next.

The pièce de résistance of Nero's circus was the alleged public consummation of one of these marriages. Yes – by consummation, we mean exactly what you think. According to some accounts, Nero took his new spouse to bed in front of guests to "prove" the marriage was real. Basically the most awkward wedding night ever, complete with spectators. True or not, the fact that people believed it tells you how far-out Nero's reputation was. This is the kind of scene even HBO might blanch at, and HBO doesn't blanch at much.

So, what do we learn from Nero's big fat gay weddings? For one, maybe keep your private life actually private – nobody wants to attend the honeymoon, not even the most supportive friend. Also, forcing a teenager to dress up as your ex-wife? Definitely on the "Don't try this at home" list (morally, legally, and in every other way). If there's any silver lining here, it's that Nero clearly didn't give a fig about traditional gender roles: he was happy being both husband and wife. Love is love, I guess – or in Nero's case, maybe narcissism is love, because he mostly seemed in love with doing whatever Nero pleased. In pop culture terms, Nero was a one-man reality show with no producers to rein him in. Take the most outrageous celebrity wedding you can imagine, multiply it by ten, throw in some crime, and remove any shame – that was Nero's approach to matrimony.

Marriage lesson from Emperor Crazy? Perhaps just that love (and lust and ego) makes people do wild things – but even by those standards, Nero is in a class of his own. And hey, maybe get mutual consent and skip the live audience when you're planning your nuptials, okay? Unlike Nero, the rest of us don't literally rule the world – so "because I said so" is not a great relationship mantra. In short: do not invite the entire city of Rome to your bedroom antics. Nero did it so we don't have to.

Holy "Matri-mony" – Saints Sergius and Bacchus

After the rollercoaster of imperial romances, let's take a holy detour to a very different kind of couple: Saints Sergius and Bacchus. Picture this: two Roman soldiers in the third century who were inseparable comrades and, if legend holds, lovers as well. In an age when being an out-and-proud Christian could get you killed (never mind being in a same-sex relationship), Sergius and Bacchus had to keep things extremely low-key. They were high-ranking officers, the elite of the Roman army – and according to later accounts, the elite of each other's hearts. If they truly were romantically involved, they managed the near-impossible: a secret love affair in the ranks of an army that was busy persecuting folks for *less*. That was double risk, double closet duty.

Sergius and Bacchus's tale unfolds during a time when Christianity was illegal in Rome, so they already had a secret (their faith) binding them together. The two were described as being as close as "brothers" – a euphemism that might have raised a few eyebrows even then. Eventually, their Christian beliefs were discovered by their superiors. That's when their story takes a painful turn. The army command tried to shame and break them: in a bizarre twist, Sergius and Bacchus were paraded through the streets in chains and women's clothing as punishment. The idea was to mock their manhood and make them feel small. (Little did their captors know, they were basically turning these two into queer icons avant la lettre – but we'll give the Romans a pass for not foreseeing that.)

The abuse didn't end with fashion humiliation. The authorities tortured them brutally. Bacchus was beaten to death first, while Sergius was forced to watch his beloved companion die. Imagine the heartbreak: your partner in love and faith is killed in front of your eyes. But this tragic love story has a supernatural twist. That night, as Sergius languished in prison, Bacchus's spirit supposedly appeared to him, radiant in a martyr's glory. Bacchus (now a literal angelic boyfriend) urged Sergius not to lose heart: *they would reunite in heaven*, where their bond could never be broken. If that isn't an eternal love declaration, what is? Buoyed by this otherworldly pep talk, Sergius endured further torture until he, too, was killed – martyring himself with Bacchus's name on his lips and the promise of heavenly reunion in his heart.

In death, Sergius and Bacchus became venerated as saints. The official church spin? Oh, they were just the *best* of friends, absolutely inseparable "brothers in Christ." (Uh-huh, we've heard that one before – roommates, right?) But many modern scholars and romantics read between the lines of their story. The devotion these two had for each other, the fact that art often depicted them together, and that Sergius reportedly had Bacchus's name on his last breath – it all hints that their bond went beyond platonic brotherhood. Some even dub them the patron saints of same-sex love – the poster boys for "just guys being dudes" who were actually much more. In some early Christian communities there was a ritual of brother-making that some interpret as a veiled form of same-sex union, and Sergius and Bacchus often get a nod as the type of pair such a ritual might have been celebrating. Controversial? Sure. But it's a heck of a compelling love story hidden in plain sight of church history.

In pop culture terms, Sergius and Bacchus are a bit like *Brokeback Mountain* meets *Gladiator*. Two warriors in love, keeping it secret under the nose of the empire, standing by each other through persecution, ultimately dying for something they believed in (and maybe also for each other). Cue the dramatic music and pass the tissues, please. The very image of two male saints who loved each other enough to face death together is both subversive and touching. They've inspired paintings, novels, and a legion of modern admirers who see in them a powerful message: that love and faith aren't mutually exclusive, and that even in an age of oppression, love finds a way (albeit a very tragic one in their case).

So what do we learn from this saintly duo? Their story shows that sharing deeply held values and having each other's back, even in adversity, can forge an unbreakable bond. They literally fought side by side, prayed side by side, and when the time came, they died side by side. One cheeky lesson: the couple that prays together, stays together… until the Roman army finds out. In more universal terms, even in the darkest times, love can be a source of strength that helps you stand tall (even if you're in shackles and a dress) against the worst the world can throw at you. Sergius and Bacchus whisper to us through history that even when love had to hide behind words like "brother" or "friend," it was still love – powerful, transformative, and very, very real.

Myth Busting Rome

Was ancient Rome basically one long pansexual toga party? Not exactly. Roman attitudes toward same-sex relationships were a mixed bag—messier than a spilled wine cup at a Roman banquet. There's a popular notion that "the ancients were totally cool with all that gay stuff." Yes and no. They didn't see sexuality the way we do. No one in ancient Rome self-identified as "gay" or "straight." It was more about roles – who was allowed to do what with whom, and in which position.

Let's lay it out: in Roman society, a male citizen was expected to be the penetrator, the top dog, so to speak, no matter the partner's gender. Being on the receiving end – especially if you were an adult male citizen – was a no-no for your reputation. The Romans were macho in the streets, freaky in the sheets, but with a ton of unwritten rules. So a senator might enthusiastically enjoy a male slave or male prostitute without anyone batting an eye; after all, he's just being a red-blooded Roman male seeking pleasure where he could. But if word got out that the same senator *preferred* being on the receiving end, oh boy, cue the derisive laughter and social shaming. That was the line you didn't cross (publicly, at least).

There were even laws like the Lex Scantinia, which supposedly punished certain male-male relations (especially involving freeborn youth). And as Christianity took hold, emperors like Constantine and his successors issued real killjoy edicts banning same-sex acts with harsh punishments. By the late Empire and Middle Ages, the laissez-faire "don't be the bottom" attitude had morphed into a strict "this is sin, repent" mandate. In other words, what was once a mild disapproval or a jokey insult became outright criminal. That infamous "closet" for hiding one's orientation largely came into existence during those later, more puritanical times.

But that's later. In the classical Roman heyday, the vibe was a peculiar mix of open secret and social tightrope. It's true that from the imperial palace to the provinces, same-sex desire was everywhere if you knew where to look. Graffiti on walls, racy art, and even love poems all attest that same-sex romance was just another part of life (even for women, though their stories got less ink).

Another myth to bust: not all Romans were chill with it. Philosophers like Cicero rolled their eyes at men who seemed *too* into other men, seeing it as a lapse in judgment. Satirists like Juvenal mocked "effeminate" males swishing around. Not everyone was exactly waving a pride flag about it. Society had its share of macho posturing and moralists wagging fingers—some things never change. Later, emperors like Constantine (and those after him) tried to legislate the bedroom once Christianity took hold, turning mild disapproval into outright criminalization. The point is, Roman society wasn't unanimously throwing confetti at same-sex couples.

Even with all those social rules, though, human nature found a way. Emperors still did their thing (occasionally in drag), poets snuck in homoerotic lines, and ordinary folks carried on. A man might flirt with a cute waiter at the tavern, or a woman might settle down with her "dear friend," and as long as no one made a fuss, life went on with all the same feelings – just no modern labels.

Were Romans uniformly tolerant? No. But they weren't as prudish as, say, Victorian England either. In many ways they were realists about sex: they knew it happened (they were a bit obsessed, honestly) and they set up quirky rules to manage it. Those rules weren't fair or equal by modern standards, but they created a space where, if you followed the decorum, you could get away with quite a bit. The real hardcore repression and closet-building came later with the moralistic turn of late antiquity.

Ancient Rome was a place where same-sex desire was an open secret. From graffiti bragging about trysts, to emperors playing house with boytoys, to soldier-saints possibly exchanging vows, the evidence is there if you look. Yet it was also a society fixated on image, masculinity, and power dynamics. They'd shrug at one scenario and scandalize at another. Hypocritical? Perhaps – but very human. Romans, like us, had their progressive moments and their deep prejudices. They celebrated love in poetry and condemned it in law, depending on the era. "When in Rome, do as the Romans" really meant navigating a complex social script — and oh, did the Romans do a lot. The closets came later, and when we peel back Rome's curtain we see a world not so different from our own: messy, scandalous, tender, tragic, and triumphant in turn. Emperor, soldier, or commoner — no matter who you were, one truth stands eternal: love (and lust) will always find a way... rules be damned.

Chapter 4

Emperors, Eunuchs, and Cut Sleeves – Queer Love in the East

The history of same-sex love isn't just the tale of secret meetings in Western castles or whisperings in Roman baths. Far from it! Across Asia – from imperial China to the courts of India – queer romance thrived, sometimes in full view of courtiers clutching their pearls (or jade, as it were). In this chapter, we journey East, where emperors snipped their robes for love, peaches became code for passion, Hindu gods swapped genders for a good time, folkloric brides said "I do" to each other, and palace concubines weren't always ladies. All of it is served with a side of humor and *OMG-did-they-really?* insight. Buckle up your brocade robes; it's going to be a fun ride through history's Eastern rainbow.

We'll meet a Chinese emperor so smitten he literally cut off his sleeve to let his boyfriend sleep in, a duke who raved about his lover's half-eaten peach like it was the latest celebrity couple trend, and Indian legends that would make even today's rom-coms blush. Along the way, expect some modern pop culture side-eyes – because what's history without connecting it to *The Real Housewives* or a K-pop idol or two? And fear not, we'll sprinkle in a few marriage lessons (or shall we say emperor advice?) gleaned from these stories – delivered with a wink and plenty of sass. Let's dive into the fabulous tales of queer love in the East, where devotion sometimes meant breaking societal norms… or just an expensive sleeve.

The Cut-Sleeve Emperor

Forget grand monuments or love songs – Emperor Ai of Han (ruling in 1st century BCE China) set the bar for romantic gestures sky high with a single snip of fabric. Picture this: the young emperor is napping in the afternoon with his favorite male companion, Dong Xian, who's using the emperor's wide sleeve as a pillow. (We've all had an arm go numb under a sleeping partner, right? Now imagine that, but you're also the *Son of Heaven* with a robe worth a kingdom.) When duty called and Emperor Ai needed to get up, did he jostle Dong Xian awake? Of course not! Instead, our love-struck emperor reaches for the scissors and cuts off his sleeve – literally freeing himself while letting his lover snooze on the royal silk. Talk about *keeping it cozy.*

This tender act became legendary, giving birth to the Chinese idiom "the passion of the cut sleeve" to describe love between men. It's arguably the most romantic wardrobe malfunction in history. If social media existed back then, #CutSleeve would be trending with captions like, "When bae's comfort means more than your drip." Emperor Ai's courtiers were so impressed (or maybe so eager to kiss up) that they reportedly started cutting one sleeve off their own robes in solidarity. Fashion statement or ancient hashtag challenge? Either way, a trend was born. Move over, Versace – Han Dynasty couture was all about that asymmetrical sleeve for a hot minute.

Now, Emperor Ai wasn't just a one-sleeve wonder; he truly doted on Dong Xian. He showered his beloved with titles, land, even made him Commander of the Armed Forces – the imperial equivalent of giving your sweetheart the keys to a sports car, a corner office, and half your company. (Marriage Lesson alert: *perhaps* don't give your S.O. control of the army, but a little spoiling never hurt.) The Emperor even moved Dong Xian's entire family into the palace and elevated them – basically turning his boyfriend into a prince overnight. Nepotism in the name of love? You bet. The other officials were *not* thrilled (imagine your boss making his partner the VP of everything – office gossip galore). But Ai didn't care; love conquered all protocol. In a modern twist, we'd say Emperor Ai was that CEO who puts his husband on the board of directors and dares anyone to object.

Of course, like many whirlwind romances, there were storm clouds on the horizon. Emperor Ai tragically died young (perhaps too much aphrodisiac, rumor says – yes, he was reportedly *that* passionate). Without his protector, poor Dong Xian was left to face jealous rivals. The new regime wasted no time stripping Dong of power and politely suggesting he take his own life – an ending more *Game of Thrones* than Disney. It's a somber footnote to an otherwise heartwarming tale. But the *legacy* of the cut sleeve lives on as a symbol of devoted love.

Marriage Lesson: True love sometimes means sacrifice – though preferably not of your limbs or couture. In everyday terms: if your partner falls asleep on your arm during movie night, maybe let them sleep and endure the pins-and-needles, or grab a scissors if you're channeling Emperor Ai (on second thought, maybe just gently adjust them!). The spirit of the cut sleeve is putting your loved one's comfort above your own. It's the ultimate "I got you, babe" move. Just ask Emperor Ai – a little less sleeve was a small price to pay for a lot of love.

The Bitten Peach

From imperial bedrooms to blossoming orchards: our next stop is ancient Wei (China, circa 6th century BCE), where a tasty piece of fruit turned into a euphemism that's *still* talked about. Enter Duke Ling of Wei, a ruler with a wife and a son, but whose heart was thoroughly stolen by a *gorgeous* male courtesan named Mizi Xia. Now, Duke Ling was proudly vocal about his love – he'd brag about Mizi Xia's beauty and devotion to anyone within earshot. (Imagine a head-over-heels billionaire posting PDA-filled Instagram stories – that was Duke Ling, only with bronze mirrors instead of smartphones.)

The lovebirds' most famous moment came during a leisurely stroll in the palace gardens. Mizi Xia plucked a perfectly ripe peach from a tree, took a bite, and – finding it exceptionally sweet – offered the remaining half to Duke Ling. Yes, he literally shared a half-eaten peach with his lover. In a world without Lady and the Tramp spaghetti dinners, this was *peak romance.* The Duke was over the moon, reportedly exclaiming, *"How sincere is your love for me! You forgot your own appetite and thought only of giving me good things to eat!"* (Cue the awww's.)

To modern ears, sharing slobbered-on fruit might not scream passion – we're conditioned to say "Ew, cooties." But in context, this was like giving someone the last slice of pizza *and* the bigger half of the cookie combined. It showed Mizi Xia cared more about his man's joy than his own snack. That simple bitten peach turned into an enduring symbol of male love in China, a poetic code for same-sex affection. Think of it as the ancient equivalent of matching couple rings or a viral #CoupleChallenge, but edible. For centuries, to speak of "love of the half-eaten peach" was to wink at the love between two men. Romantic and dietary all at once!

Now, if this were a Hollywood movie, the credits would roll on the Duke and Mizi Xia kissing under a peach tree, happily ever after. But history, alas, loves a twist. Fast forward a bit: Mizi Xia's beauty fades with time (as beauty tends to do unless you're, say, *Paul Rudd*). Duke Ling's ardor cools. And here comes the jaw-dropper – the Duke not only falls out of love; he revises their history with audacious pettiness. He has the nerve to complain, "Ugh, that guy *stole my carriage* that one time and had the gall to give me a gnawed peach!" Yes, Mr. "How sweet, you thought of me!" did a total 180: now he's painting the once-adorable peach gift as some rude affront. Talk about rewriting the relationship narrative – the Duke would fit right in on a reality TV reunion special, throwing shade after the breakup.

This part of the story is often left out in the retellings (because it's a downer), but ancient philosopher Han Feizi recorded it as a warning: *royal favor is fickle, darling.* One minute you're the apple (or peach) of his eye, the next you're persona non grata. If Duke Ling were alive today, Mizi Xia would be subtweeting about him, and the Duke would be the subject of a thousand angry tweets calling out his hypocrisy (#PeachGate, anyone?).

Yet, for all that drama, the term "bitten peach" endured as a positive emblem of love. It outlived both the Duke's change of heart and Mizi Xia's moment in the sun. In a way, it's poetic justice: Duke Ling's name is mud compared to the sweet, juicy symbol of the love he once celebrated. People remember the peach, not the petty.

Marriage Lesson: Share your goodies with your beloved – be it dessert or life's delights – but also, beware of fair-weather lovers. Consistency is key! If someone *praised* your half-eaten peach in private, they shouldn't later trash you for it in public. True love means owning the story even when the sugar rush of infatuation wears off. And if you ever find yourself dating a powerful figure, keep receipts (figuratively speaking) – you never know when history might need your side of the story. In simpler terms: love deeply like Mizi Xia, but maybe don't put *all* your peaches in one basket.

Kama Sutra's Cousins

Meanwhile, in the ancient lands of South Asia, love and desire were getting about as genre-bending and flamboyant as a Bollywood awards show – with gods and heroes playing musical chairs with gender and sexuality. Think ancient India was all prudish and repressed? Oh honey, have a seat (preferably a lotus position) and let's enlighten you. The same culture that gave the world the Kama Sutra – that famous guide to lovemaking – had no shortage of queer tales and *divine* dalliances. In fact, Indian epics and mythology are so LGBTQ-friendly by modern standards that one might wonder how Victorian Brits who colonized India clutched their pearls hard enough to leave permanent indentations.

Let's drop some names: Mahabharata and Ramayana, the massive epic sagas that are basically the superhero crossover events of ancient India, both feature characters who'd fit right in at a Pride parade. In the Mahabharata, we meet Shikhandi, born a princess, later living as a man (long story short: a sex change via a supernatural Yaksha loaner – eat your heart out, *Pose*). Shikhandi is a trans hero(ine) who literally changes the tide of war. There's also Arjuna, one of the main heroes, who spends a portion of exile disguised as a woman (teaching dance and music in a royal harem, no less!). We could say he got in touch with his feminine side – *very* in touch, rocking bangles and braid as Brihannala for a year. Gender fluid much?

Then there's the poignant tale of Aravan (also called Iravan). Facing sacrifice in battle, Aravan had one last wish: to experience marriage. No women were keen to marry a man doomed to die the next day (understandably a bummer for honeymoon plans). So what happens? Lord Krishna – the ultimate cosmic trickster – says, "No bro shall die a bachelor on my watch," and promptly transforms into Mohini, a beautiful female form, to wed Aravan for a night. They marry, share a tender night, and the next day Aravan goes heroically to his end. Widowed Mohini-Krishna then mourns him in full widow attire. This tale is so revered that, to this day, some communities in India (notably the transgender Hijra community) commemorate Aravan's story in annual festivals, re-enacting the mystical marriage. It's like *A Midsummer Night's Dream* meets *Braveheart*, with a dash of RuPaul.

And how about the gods themselves? Shiva, the macho destroyer deity, and Vishnu, the preserver (who, as we saw, isn't shy about dragging up as Mohini), have a story that's the stuff of tantric legend. When Vishnu is in his seductively divine Mohini form, Shiva is so smitten he chases "her" down and, ahem, they unite. Depending on the version, this union produces a son – godly DNA is wild, y'all. One popular outcome is the birth of Ayyappa, a deity who literally has two dads (well, one dad and one gender-fluid dad/mom – pronouns get complicated when you're a god). Also, let's not forget

Ardhanarishvara, the composite form of Shiva united with his wife Parvati in one body, half male, half female – talk about non-binary iconography! This figure says in cosmic form, "Hey, we contain multitudes – male and female in one. Deal with it." The Hindu pantheon was out here serving gender inclusivity and duality as sacred truth millennia ago, basically dropping truth bombs that gender is a spectrum and even deities are *versatile*.

Historically, this acceptance of fluid love wasn't just in myths. Ancient Indian society recognized a category loosely translated as the "third gender" (today we'd say trans or non-binary folks). They were called hijras or other local terms, and while not always treated as equals (let's be real, patriarchy spared no one), they often had respected roles – like blessing newborns or marriages, or serving in royal courts. The Kama Sutra itself (compiled around the 3rd century CE) has entire sections acknowledging same-sex behaviors. Surprise! The famous handbook on lovemaking includes guidance for male-male oral sex and mentions men who act as women in relationships (and vice versa). In other words, the Kama Sutra basically said, "There are all kinds of folks and all kinds of pleasure – you do you (or do *each other*)." No big moral panic attached.

So if ancient South Asia was relatively chill about all this, where did the notion that queer love is "against Indian/Asian culture" come from? Two words: Colonial Prudery – that fun era when the British showed up with their Victorian sensibilities and anti-sodomy laws and said "Tsk tsk, none of that, you heathens." They outlawed homosexual acts in the 19th century (Section 377 of the penal code, if you want the receipt), and generally spread their uptight vibes across the land. Ironically, these were the same Brits whose own King James I had male favorites and whose elite read ancient Greek man-love poetry in Latin class – but hey, *hypocrisy* is the original imperial export. Overnight, centuries of a more easygoing attitude were painted over by imported homophobia. Love that once dared speak its name (in Sanskrit, Persian, Tamil, take your pick) had to go underground.

But guess what? Culture has a way of remembering. The stories persisted in grandma's folktales, in temple art showing two women embracing, in sly jokes and idioms. And in recent years, countries like India have started shedding those colonial hangovers – in 2018, India's Supreme Court finally decriminalized homosexuality, effectively saying "So sorry about that Victorian chapter, carry on with the love, folks."

Marriage Lesson: The old tales of Shiva and Vishnu, of Shikhandi and Aravan, remind us that love and gender have never been one-size-fits-all. Sometimes your soulmate comes in a form society didn't expect – *the gods certainly didn't mind!* If the cosmos can accommodate a transgender warrior, a god who's part woman, or two queens making a baby (oh, did we mention King Bhagiratha? In one legend, this great king – ancestor of Rama – was born to two widowed queens who made love to each other with divine blessing. Yup, a baby with two moms in a 14th-century tale!). The universe clearly endorses creative expressions of love. So the lesson is: Embrace love in its many forms and don't let anyone tell you it isn't "traditional" – often, it's more traditional than the traditions that forgot it. And to any couple feeling ostracized, just remember you've got literal deities on your side who've been there, done that, and got the epic poem to prove it.

Two Brides for a Baba (Folklore)

Now for a story that sounds like a Shakespeare comedy crossed with a progressive fairy tale – with a dash of ghostly intervention just for kicks. This gem comes from Rajasthani folklore in India, and it's all about two brides who end up married… to each other. (Accidental lesbian wedding in medieval India? Yes, indeed – and you thought *Ellen and Portia* were trailblazers.)

Once upon a time in a Rajasthani village, there lived a wealthy merchant (a Seth) who desperately wanted a son. When a daughter was born – let's call her Beeja – he said "Eh, close enough," and raised her as a boy anyway. Beeja grew up wearing turbans, riding horses, and probably perfecting that confident swagger – think *Mulan*, but instead of saving China, she's running the family business in disguise. So convincing was the charade that another local family arranged to marry their lovely daughter Teeja to this "fine young man" Beeja. (Talk about a *Big Fat Indian Wedding* twist – the groom's a woman in drag, unbeknownst to the bride's family. You can practically hear the drumroll for drama.)

Wedding day arrives with the usual pomp: elephants, fireworks, aunties gossiping. Teeja and Beeja tie the knot, still none the wiser about each other's biology under all those layers of silk and jewelry. It's on the wedding night, according to the tale, that the truth comes out. We can imagine the scene: two nervous young people, an elaborate bed with flowers, both expecting *something* and then – "Wait… you're a girl?! I'm a girl! OMG!" Talk about an awkward meet-cute.

Now, you'd think this would end in chaos – families shouting, annulment papers flying. But here's the beautiful kicker: Teeja and Beeja decide, *so what if we're both women?* They care for each other (they'd struck up a friendship as "husband and wife," after all) and they jointly say, "To heck with society's rules, we're staying married and making this work!" Instead of going back to the mandap and demanding refunds on the gifts, these two brides basically run off together, hand-in-hand, into the wilderness to live life on their own terms. (The village must have been shook. Two brides without a groom? Who's going to explain this to Grandma?!)

But wait, there's more – a folktale always has a dash of magic. As Teeja and Beeja set up home together, along comes the King of Ghosts (because why not) who offers Beeja a boon: "I can turn you into a man, if that'll help smooth things over." Ah, the well-intentioned ghost trying to play fairy godmother! Beeja, now thinking practically, says "Sure, let's try that," and *poof* – she's physically transformed into a man. You'd assume this is the happily-ever-after moment (now they fit the societal mold, problem solved!). But in a delicious twist, this magical sex change nearly wrecks their relationship. The lore hints that once Beeja became male, the dynamics changed – perhaps Beeja started acting like a *typical guy* of that era, with all the entitlement that entails, or maybe Teeja missed the tender way things were when they were two women in it together. Whatever the case, the couple hits a rough patch. It turns out that they loved each other as women, and forcing them into the conventional husband-wife template wasn't the answer. (Hear that, Ghost King? Keep your boons to yourself next time.)

Realizing this, Beeja ultimately reverts to being a woman (folklore logic: if a ghost can turn you one way, a ghost can turn you back!). Teeja's like, "Thank god, I liked you better this way." They resume their life as two wives, living happily ever after far away from those judgy villagers. The story, often known as *"Dohri Zindagi"* ("Double Life") or *"A New Life"*, has been retold by storytellers and even modern writers because its message was ahead of its time: love is love, and it's the world around you that might need to adjust.

Is this not the plot of the coolest Netflix period drama we haven't seen yet? It's got everything: social satire, heartfelt romance, supernatural shenanigans, and a big "screw you" to rigid gender roles. One can almost imagine a comedic scene where Teeja and Beeja return to the village for supplies and some nosy neighbor asks, "So where's your husband?" and they glance at each other like, "Which one of us should answer that?" In a conservative society, their very existence was revolutionary. If there were tabloids then, the headline would be: *"Runaway Brides Defy Custom – Start Alternative Family Unit, Ghost Involved"*.

Marriage Lesson: This folktale serves up a great one: the strongest relationships are built on authenticity and equality. Teeja and Beeja tried the "let's fit in" approach (literally shape-shifting to conform), and it nearly tanked their love. When they embraced their true selves, *that's* when they thrived. In modern terms: don't change who you are just to make others comfortable. The right partner will love the real you and stand by you against the naysayers – even if it means moving to a new town or facing down a disapproving auntie brigade. Also, fine print: parents, maybe don't deceive an entire village by cross-dressing your kid for years; it's not a sustainable long-term plan. But if life does land you in a queer situation (pun fully intended), honesty and love can find a way. Teeja and Beeja's story is basically the original "love wins" – with a paranormal twist – and we are so here for it.

Courts and Concubines

By now it's clear that from peasants to princes, nobody in Eastern history had a monopoly on same-sex love. But we'd be remiss not to dish about the *big leagues* – the royal courts, where power, politics, and passion collided in high drama worthy of a dozen opera plots. Think your workplace has gossip? Honey, an imperial court was like TMZ, Dynasty, and The Crown combined, especially when emperors and sultans took male lovers or *ahem* "special friends." In Eastern empires, many a throne was kept warm not just by queens and empresses, but by dashing young men who caught the monarch's eye. Let's spill the tea.

Take the Han Dynasty of China – we've met Emperor Ai and his sleeve, but he was far from an outlier. In fact, out of the dozen Western Han emperors, the majority had male companions alongside their empresses. The historian Sima Qian even wrote a whole chapter about these male favorites, basically an ancient VIP list of the emperor's boyfriends. (Imagine a section in an official state history titled "The Emperor's Male Lovers" – that's how normalized it was at the top.) One early Han emperor, Gaozu (Liu Bang) – a rough-and-tumble founder of the dynasty – loved a eunuch named Ji Ru so much that during one military crisis, Gaozu hid in the bedroom with Ji Ru for TEN days, ignoring his generals. Talk about *priorities*. The empire is burning, but the emperor is like, "brb, busy cuddling." When a furious general finally barged in, he found the emperor literally lounging on Ji Ru's lap. If that isn't the ancient Chinese version of "not now, I'm on bae-cation," I don't know what is.

Then Gaozu's heir, Emperor Hui, had a fave named Hongru who was so influential that courtiers started imitating his style – wearing their hats and belts like Hongru, even dabbing on a bit of rouge maybe. Essentially, Emperor Hui's court became *Hongru Fan Club HQ*. (Picture if the U.S. Cabinet all started dressing like the president's stylish boyfriend – it was like that.) One anecdote relates how Hongru's influence even saved a life: the Emperor's mom didn't like one of his decisions and threatened Hongru via a messenger, saying, "If my boy kills my favorite, I'll kill yours" – yikes! Hongru, savvy and probably a bit shaken, convinced Emperor Hui to chill out on said execution. Thus, the imperial boy-toy doubled as a political negotiator. Not just arm candy, but actually steering affairs of state between pillow sessions. Talk about multitasking.

Chinese history is replete with such tales: Emperor Wen of Han had *three* handsome male lovers (two were eunuchs-turned-chariot drivers and one lucky commoner who got promoted because the emperor literally dreamed he should – yes, a dream hookup leading to real-life favor). The trend continued on and off through later dynasties. Many emperors bestowed riches and titles on their male favorites, provoking envy in bureaucrats who had been slogging through Confucian exams only to see Boyfriend #1 leapfrog them to power. The trope of the "corrupting favorite" appears often – though one could argue the emperors were just living their best lives. Eunuchs, by the way, often became go-betweens or even lovers themselves. Since they were castrated, emperors trusted them with the harem and other sensitive roles, but that didn't mean eunuchs lacked intimacy. Some formed relationships with women of the palace (safe liaison since eunuchs can't impregnate) and others with fellow eunuchs or courtiers. So yes, the Forbidden City had its own web of romances – a bit like a high-stakes soap opera where everyone's wearing silk slippers and plotting intrigue in flowery language.

Now slide over to South Asia's courts. The grand Mughal Empire in India, famed for the Taj Mahal and spicy curries, had its share of same-sex saga in the palace. We already mentioned Babur, the first Mughal emperor, who as a young prince wrote heart-throbbing poetry about a beautiful boy back in his homeland. Picture teenage Babur, future conqueror of Delhi, wandering the bazaar of Samarkand lovestruck, composing couplets about Baburi (the boy's name even sounds like a pet version of Babur – coincidence? I think not). Babur literally compared his infatuation to the legendary love of *Majnun* for *Laila* (a classic heterosexual love story), basically saying, "I'm as crazy in love as that guy, even though my crush is a dude." It's kind of adorable – history's ferocious warlord was at heart a romantic poet with a hopeless crush. (If only he'd had access to late-night WhatsApp or TikTok, Babur might've sent Baburi some cringe DMs and saved himself some heartache.)

As the Mughal dynasty rolled on, accounts pop up of emperors and princes getting *very* fond of handsome male servants, dancers, or warriors. The Mughal courts, much like the Persian courts before them, appreciated youthful male beauty in art and verse. Urdu and Persian poetry of the time is chock-full of admiration for the "gulam" or cup-bearer, usually a comely boy serving wine. Poets like Sa'di and Hafiz (Persian, slightly earlier) wrote ghazals so steamy about the gaze of a male wine-server that you'd blush. This tradition carried into Mughal India – heck, even *before* the Mughals, some Delhi Sultans had reputations for enjoying the company of pretty boys. The Delhi Sultan Alauddin Khilji in the 13th century had a famous general, Malik Kafur, who was a gorgeous enslaved eunuch he fell for. Khilji elevated Kafur to be essentially second-in-command of the empire. Rumors flew that Kafur had the Sultan wrapped around his finger (or whichever appendage, *ahem*). That bromance/romance ended badly – palace intrigue, assassinations – but it left an imprint: the idea that a skilled, charming man could rise from nothing to power via the Sultan's affections. Sound familiar? That script played out in many courts, not just Khilji's.

Meanwhile, in later centuries, Nawabs (provincial kings) of places like Lucknow were patronizing male dancers and theatre performers, sometimes blurring lines between art and amour. The Nawab of Oudh, Wajid Ali Shah, for instance, was known for his love of dance and drama; he even performed female roles himself and kept company of *all sorts* of creative souls. He wasn't chastised for any implied queerness as much as for, say, losing his kingdom to the British. Priorities, you know. In princely India, having a male favorite was often just seen as part of a ruler's indulgences, like having an extra dessert. Sure, tut-tuts might ensue, especially if it affected governance, but it wasn't the scandal *Victorian England* would make it out to be.

Zooming out, across Persia and the wider Islamic world, it was similar: many rulers had harems of women and also enjoyed male companions. They even institutionalized it in some places – the young male courtiers (often called ghilman or catamites by chroniclers) were sometimes trained to entertain and please. Not exactly consensual by modern standards, but it was a facet of court life. Poetry from those courts often doesn't shy away from homoerotic imagery. One famous poet, Abu Nuwas of 9th-century Baghdad, wrote odes to wine and boys that would make a sailor blush, yet he was celebrated for it (and also occasionally jailed because he partied *that* hard). So from the Middle East to South Asia to East Asia, same-sex love frequently strutted the corridors of power in silk robes, even if later prudish historians tried to sweep it under the imperial rug.

Marriage Lesson: If there's one thing these courtly capers teach us, it's that relationships can be complicated – especially when power is involved. Love can elevate (see: commoners turned royal favorites) but also corrupt (see: jealous courtiers, political fallout, occasionally poison in the wine). For us common folk, the takeaway might be: don't mix your professional power dynamics with your love life if you can help it – HR would not approve, and neither would the royal chroniclers. But more universally: love is a great equalizer. Emperor or servant, Nawab or dancer, the heart wants what it wants. And despite the risks, many throughout history followed their hearts anyway, leaving us these incredible stories.

From Emperor Ai's cut sleeve to Mizi Xia's peach, from the queer pantheon of Hindu myth to two village girls thumbing their noses at gender norms, and all those scheming palace boyfriends in between – one truth stands out: same-sex love is no modern fad or Western import, it's a tale as old as time and as Asian as tea. These stories are as much a part of Eastern heritage as dragons and spice. They show humanity in all its diversity, having a laugh, shedding a tear, making *really* questionable decisions for love (looking at you, Emperor Ai's tailors). And through these tales runs a humorous, defiant thread: love and desire will bloom in the unlikeliest places, often right under the noses of those who say "it's not our culture." History winks back, *Oh, it absolutely was.*

So the next time someone claims LGBT relationships are "new" or "foreign," feel free to serve them some history with a side of sass: tell them about the emperor who was so whipped he ruined his outfit, the king who enjoyed a pre-chewed peach, the god who became a goddess to marry a man, or the two desi girls who married and outsmarted a ghost. The past is full of pride – and a lot of it is frankly hilarious and heartwarming. In the grand story of love, our Eastern ancestors were out here breaking rules and having fun doing it. As the saying might go, fashions change, empires fall, but the passion of the cut sleeve endures – and ain't that a fabulous thing?

Chapter 5

Monks, Moors & Medieval Mysteries – Same-Sex Secrets of the Middle Ages

It turns out the so-called Dark Ages had more colorful love lives than the legends let on. Yes, while knights jousted and monks chanted, some of them were also penning love letters, sharing beds, and whispering sweet nothings in Latin or Arabic. Get ready for a journey through medieval same-sex capers that would make even a modern gossip columnist blush. We'll explore convent confessions, royal bromances, poetic rhapsodies from Baghdad, "brotherly" bonds in Byzantium, and finally bust some myths about medieval sexuality. Grab your quill and let's dive in – with a wink and a nudge – into the untold queer secrets of the Middle Ages.

Cloistered Crushes – Passionate letters between 12th-century nuns reveal "hauntingly beautiful" love poems of one sister for another

Imagine a silent medieval convent somewhere in 12th-century Europe. By day, it's all prayer and chores. By night, under the soft glow of a tallow candle, one nun sits on her cot, heart pounding, writing a letter that would *definitely* not get Mother Superior's approval. This isn't your typical "dear sister in Christ" correspondence – it's more like a medieval love letter that could give today's romance novels a run for their money. Forget courtly knights and damsels; here we have cloistered crushes unfolding between sisters of the cloth.

One such letter survives, and it's *juicy*. In it, a nun pours out her soul to another nun in language so tender and poetic you'd think Shakespeare snuck into the monastery early. "I sigh for you at every hour, at every moment, like a hungry little bird," she writes wistfully, comparing her longing to a dove that's lost its mate. Hauntingly beautiful? Absolutely – our lovelorn sister basically invented the slow-burn love poem centuries before Hallmark got in the game. She goes on to recall "the kisses you gave, and the words of joy with which you caressed my little breasts" – yes, she wrote that in a *letter*! (Take that, *Bridgerton*.) Every line drips with yearning: her beloved's absence makes the world colorless; her speeches are "sweet beyond honey and honeycomb," and even gold and silver seem dull next to the shine of this forbidden love.

If you're picturing a stern abbess reading this and doing a spit-take with her morning ale, you're not alone. How did these letters get exchanged? Enter the convent's version of sneaky DMs: trusted messengers or maybe a friendly monk who thought he was just delivering innocent sisterly correspondence. Little did he know he was basically medieval Cupid's mailman. One can only hope he didn't peek, or he might have needed confession *himself* after reading those sensuous lines.

The tone of these letters is passionate and surprisingly frank. Our nun doesn't just deal in spiritual metaphors – she flat-out professes love with "soul and body." It's like reading a secret diary where the ink itself blushes. Keep in mind, these women were brides of Christ officially – sworn to chastity and all that jazz. But hey, love finds a way, even in a cloister locked tighter than a king's treasury. When human touch and companionship are denied, the heart sometimes substitutes with the nearest acceptable outlet – in this case, a dear friend who becomes much more than a friend. It's the ultimate forbidden love trope, but it happened in real life under those wimples and veils.

Modern analogies? Think of a girls' boarding school romance, like a medieval version of *Blue Is the Warmest Color*, but with parchment instead of texting and wimples instead of blue hair. Or imagine two pop stars collaborating on a secret love song that never gets released because their managers wouldn't approve – that's how covert these sisterly love notes had to be. They wrote in flowery language and biblical references as cover. (If you get caught, just say "Oh, those honey and honeycomb lines? Totally about Jesus!" Sure, sister, sure.)

Marriage lesson hidden in this tale: even if you've taken what is essentially a lifelong vow of singleness, the human need for love and connection doesn't evaporate. Emotional intimacy can flourish in the unlikeliest places. If two nuns in a medieval convent could keep their love alive through letters passed under the cell door, then modern couples can definitely survive a little time apart with only WhatsApp and Zoom at their disposal! And they knew the power of sweet words – a good reminder that sending your significant other a random love note (or text) can make their day... just maybe avoid comparing them to a turtle-dove on a dried-up branch, that one might need some context.

As our love-struck sister ends one letter, she prays "bitter death may not come before I enjoy the sight of you again." It's part prayer, part plea, and wholly dramatic – basically the medieval nun version of "I can't live if living is without you." (Cue the power ballad!) It gives us a window into a hidden world of same-sex affection that flourished in shadows long before anyone had terms like "lesbian" or "queer." They simply called it friendship in public, but these letters reveal it was oh so much more in private.

So, the next time someone assumes nuns are married only to Jesus, remind them that Sister So-and-So might have had a secret sweetheart on the side – a fellow nun who traded verses of the Song of Songs with her like love notes. It's equal parts heartwarming and heartbreaking: heartwarming because love bloomed in a harsh place, heartbreaking because it had to remain a secret sealed with wax and hidden in Latin prose. Yet, from these cloistered walls, the universal story shines through: love laughs at locksmiths – or in this case, at abbey gates.

And speaking of love laughing at locks… moving out of the convent and into the castle, let's talk about two kings who got *very* cozy, making the rumor mill of Christendom work overtime.

Knights in Shining… Love – King Richard the Lionheart shared a bed (and perhaps more) with King Philip of France. A Crusader sleepover that launched rumors across Christendom

Royal bromance alert! Picture it: the 12th century's two most eligible bachelors – Richard the Lionheart of England and Philip II of France – forming an alliance. How do two alpha kings seal a political deal? A formal treaty? A chivalrous handshake? Pfft, too basic. These two decided to literally get into bed together. (Talk about a special relationship!) It was the medieval equivalent of a diplomatic sleepover, and you better believe people gossiped about it from London to Jerusalem.

Chroniclers of the time were basically the TMZ of the Middle Ages, and one reported that Richard and Philip "ate every day at the same table and from the same dish, and at night their beds did not separate them." *Cue spit-take.* Even King Henry II (Richard's dad) was apparently astonished at how close his boy had gotten to the French monarch. Imagine Papa Henry's face: "I wanted you two to get along, but not *that* well!" It's like a father walking in to find his son and the neighbor kid having a sleepover in the same sleeping bag – a bit beyond the usual bromance.

Now, to be fair to medieval history, sharing a bed wasn't always loaded with innuendo back then. Sometimes a bed was just a bed (and a good way to stay warm in drafty castles). But let's get real: when two kings do it, tongues wag. These guys could afford separate chambers in separate palaces, yet here they are, cuddled up under the same royal blanket. Even in a time when dudes being bros was an art form (think knights hugging after battle, or the whole knightly "brother-in-arms" thing), Richard and Philip's *extra* closeness stood out. It was a political statement, sure – a big old "France and England are BFFs now" announcement – but many wondered if there was a more… personal chemistry at play.

The Crusader sleepover happened around 1187, when Richard (still a prince at that point) was visiting Philip's court. The story goes that they shared a bed as a symbol of unity after negotiating an alliance. Medieval photo op, anyone? It's like if two presidents today skipped the joint press conference and posted a TikTok of themselves sharing a hotel suite's king-size bed, declaring "No homo–just diplomacy, folks!" Good luck with that PR spin. Naturally, medieval chroniclers wrote it up with a wink and a nudge. They didn't have the term "bromance," but if they did, it would have been splashed in Gothic calligraphy all over the manuscripts.

In the ensuing years, Richard and Philip went off on the Third Crusade together – the ultimate road trip for our knightly duo. It had all the makings of a buddy movie: they fought side by side, probably bickered like an old married couple about strategy, and caused scandalized whispers whenever seen in close conference. Some rumors hinted that Richard's preference for male company went beyond Philip – apparently he had faves among his knights too, rewarding certain handsome companions with prime positions (in the military... *wink*). Philip, for his part, married a Danish princess, but people noted he didn't rush into that and seemed pretty torn up when Richard was captured by the Germans on the way back from Crusade. (Yes, our English King got kidnapped – medieval politics was *wild* – and Philip's response was basically, "Oh no, what a shame... BTW, let's invade his lands while he's jailed." Hell hath no fury like a French king scorned? Their bromance did sour when political chips were down.)

Modern pop culture analogy: this is like if Captain America (Richard) and Iron Man (Philip) had a brief period of being *too* fond of each other, then fell out, then got back together when aliens invaded (okay, substitute "Saladin's armies" for aliens). Or think of Richard and Philip as the medieval Brothers from another mother – except one day one brother decides he wants the top bunk AND the other's toys. Maybe they were lovers, maybe just super intense BFFs; either way, their dynamic was compelling enough that medieval historians couldn't stop talking about it. If Twitter existed then, #RichPhil would be trending with speculation memes.

Of course, back then you couldn't openly accuse kings of being *that way* without losing your head (or at least your tongue). But the chroniclers found a sly workaround: just report the strangely intimate facts and let readers draw their own conclusions. "Loved him as his own soul," one account says – an innocent phrasing on the surface (David and Jonathan from the Bible, anyone?) yet *dripping* with subtext for those who read between the lines. It's almost comical how they set the scene: dining together (aww cute date), sharing a bed (scandalous!), startling the King of England (the medieval equivalent of "the parents found out!"). This story had legs, and it's been skipping through history books ever since.

Marriage lesson or rather *relationship lesson* from this royal saga? Well, if your partner starts spending every night at their "friend's" house and publicly sharing meals from the same plate with them, you might want to have a chat. Also, mixing business and pleasure – tricky even for kings. Richard and Philip's alliance turned into a lovers' quarrel on an international scale once the honeymoon phase (read: initial Crusade victories) was over. Perhaps the modern takeaway: communication is key. Maybe if they'd had couples counseling (mediated by the Pope, perhaps), England and France could've avoided a lot of drama! But seriously, this tale reminds us that even the mightiest aren't immune to personal entanglements. Work wives/husbands are a thing, and in this case, the work husbands nearly changed the course of European history with their camaraderie (or whatever one might call it).

As the rumors of Richard and Philip's great affection flew, so did the backlash. Clergymen tut-tutted about sodomy, nobles chuckled into their goblets, and troubadours probably made a baldy joke or two in the taverns (perhaps an R-rated ballad lost to time). Yet, despite whispers of scandal, Richard's reputation as a warrior-king remained solid – apparently slaying Saracens overshadowed snuggling with Frenchmen. And when Richard lay on his deathbed years later (from a battlefield wound, not a broken heart), guess who sent a courteous note of condolence? King Philip, that old softie.

From bedfellows to battlefield bros, Richard and Philip's relationship shows the fine line between political alliance and love story. And it's a reminder that history isn't just dates and battles – it's also people and the juicy, messy relationships between them. If two crusading kings can blur the lines of friendship, imagine what else was going on behind the heavy tapestries of palaces and churches.

Speaking of behind tapestries, while Europe had its clandestine royal love stories, the medieval Islamic world was composing poetry about beautiful boys and indulging in a very open kind of secret. Let's swing (pun intended) over to the Middle East, where wine, verse, and same-sex crushes flowed freely in the Golden Age…

Sultans of Swing (Both Ways) – In the Islamic Golden Age, poets like Abu Nuwas in Baghdad sang of wine, boys, and beauty. Caliphs and viziers often had male companions, and love poems to handsome youths were the rage.

Welcome to 9th-century Baghdad – a city of glittering mosques, thriving scholarship, and apparently some pretty wild parties if you knew the right people. While in Europe monks were laboring over illuminated manuscripts, in the Islamic Golden Age poets were penning odes to wine and handsome boys that would make a modern nightclub owner raise an eyebrow. If medieval Baghdad had tabloids, the cover story might read something like: *"Caliph's Court Poet Scandalizes with Homoerotic Hits – Youthful Cupbearer Inspires Latest Ode."*

The star of this scene? Abu Nuwas – think of him as the rockstar poet of his day. This guy was *unapologetic.* He wrote poems celebrating drinking (lots of drinking) and the charms of both women and men, especially young men. In one famous poem, he basically brags about the delights of the bath-house, where (to paraphrase) *"the mysteries hidden by trousers are revealed".* Yes, he went there over a thousand years ago. No subtle euphemisms, no coy blushing – Abu Nuwas was outright ogling the cute guy across the steam room and putting it into high art. If there had been a medieval Instagram, he'd post a thirst trap with a verse caption and not even use a filter.

How did he get away with this in a culture often stereotyped as strict? Well, the Abbasid Caliphate's elite had a taste for the finer things – including things that officially the religion frowned upon. Imagine a society where the religious law says "no wine, no same-sex antics," but the upper crust is basically having an extended Gatsby party behind palace walls. It's hypocrisy, sure, but also human nature. The caliphs and their entourage operated by a sort of Vegas rule: what happens in the palace, stays in the palace (until a poet publishes a juicy verse about it).

Abu Nuwas's poems about "forbidden love" (forbidden by clerics, at least) were wildly popular. They were the medieval equivalent of top 40 hits – recited in courts, shared in salons. One of his recurring characters is the young wine boy – the charming lad who serves you wine and steals your heart (and maybe more) in the process. He writes about gazing into the boy's eyes as he pours the wine, mixing intoxication with infatuation. It's heady stuff. If you swapped the goblet for a cocktail, it could be a scene in a James Bond film – the suave hero flirting with a hot bartender – except here the hero and bartender are both dudes in a society that publicly pretends not to approve. Scandalous, you say? The audience ate it up like baklava.

Now, it wasn't just poets who were into male companionship. Caliphs and viziers – the big bosses of the realm – often kept attractive male slaves or courtiers for, let's say, "company." One caliph, Muhammad al-Amin (son of the famous Harun al-Rashid), was so smitten with his boy toys that he kind of neglected the whole "produce an heir" business. Oops. He had a harem full of women (as expected of a ruler) but word on the street was he didn't pay the ladies much attention. Instead, he spent his time with his male lovers, even having his concubines dress up as young males to try to get him interested. (Picture the palace wardrobe department scrambling: "Fetch the fake beards and men's robes, the Caliph's coming!") If that isn't commitment to a preference, I don't know what is. Ultimately his lack of an heir and general hedonism contributed to his downfall – but hey, he lived his truth until politics caught up with him. One might quip that Al-Amin was the original "out-and-proud" royal, albeit within the safety of his very privileged bubble. Had Instagram been around, perhaps he'd have filled his story with selfies lounging with his favorite boys, hashtag #LivingMyBestLife #NoBabiesNoProblem.

And it wasn't just Baghdad. Over in Al-Andalus (medieval Spain under Muslim rule), poets like Ibn Quzman and others also wrote saucy verses flirting with male and female subjects alike. The Islamic world's literati had a reputation for swinging both ways in poetry; it was almost expected that a truly cultured gentleman could appreciate beauty in *all* forms. Think of it as an sophisticated affectation: "Oh yes, I am so cultured I can admire the curve of a young man's cheek and the curl of his mustache *and* praise a woman's beauty in the next line." Versatility was in vogue.

This isn't to say everyone was cool with it. As always, the more conservative types clutched their prayer beads and grumbled about sin and morality. Sometimes Abu Nuwas himself got into trouble – there are accounts of him being jailed for blasphemy or for going a bit too far with his sharp tongue. But he'd bounce back, pen another zinger of a poem, and continue being the wild child of classical Arabic literature. His legacy endured: to this day calling someone "Abu Nuwas" in parts of the Middle East hints they might be fond of drink or of, well, the kind of love Abu Nuwas loved.

Pop culture analogy: Abu Nuwas is like a blend of Oscar Wilde and Prince – witty, scandalous, gloriously uninhibited about his same-sex desires, and a favorite of the elite until he pushed the envelope *too* far. And the Caliph with his male harem? He's a bit like a medieval

Elton John throwing lavish parties – except imagine if Elton also ran an empire and had to occasionally pretend he cared about traditional family values. Awkward!

Relationship insight: Interestingly, in many of these poems, love is love – sometimes the poet writes to a woman, sometimes to a man, and the rapture and heartache sound equally convincing. It's a reminder that regardless of gender, the core emotions of love – the joy, the jealousy, the morning-after remorse when you've had too much wine – are universal. The medieval Muslim world's poets didn't label themselves; they just indulged in the full spectrum of attraction with a poetic shrug. Perhaps a lesson there is: be true to your feelings and you might create something beautiful (just maybe don't expect the religious authorities to give you high-fives for it).

As for the marriage lesson here: if your spouse is a powerful ruler who isn't showing interest in you but is throwing wine parties with pretty young things every night, your relationship might need work… or a miracle. (Case in point: one Caliph's wife supposedly resorted to hiring relationship "consultants" – in this case, cross-dressing handmaidens – to lure her husband's attention. Modern version: hiring a marriage counselor or, heck, role-playing. Desperate times, desperate measures across the ages!).

So yes, the Islamic Golden Age had a golden *rainbow* lining. Poets and potentates alike explored same-sex love in their own ways – sometimes privately, sometimes in verses for all to see. It was at once widely acknowledged in culture and officially denied in religion – a duality that, frankly, still exists in many places today. The more things change, the more they stay the same, huh?

Now, while caliphs were busy with poetry and palatial companions, back in Christian Europe a very curious practice was taking place: a church-approved ceremony that sounds an awful lot like a medieval same-sex wedding… if you squint a little. Time to talk about "brotherly love" going literal.

Brother-Making and Bosom Buddies – The Eastern Orthodox rite of "adelphopoiesis" (brother-making) has raised eyebrows – some historians think these church ceremonies bonded men in something akin to marital unions.

In the grand theater of medieval Christianity, the official party line was "marriage is one man, one woman (and ideally no funny business)." But in the Byzantine East, they seem to have slipped a sneaky loophole into the program. It was called adelphopoiesis, a Greek tongue-twister meaning "brother-making." On paper, it was a ceremony to join two men (occasionally two women, but usually men) in spiritual brotherhood. In practice… well, some suspect it was the church's *Don't Ask, Don't Tell* version of a civil union. Because nothing says "just pals" like exchanging vows and embracing in front of an altar, right?

Let's set the scene: two medieval dudes stand in a candlelit church, before a robed priest. The atmosphere is solemn, incense swirling, an icon of some famous pair of male saints – say, Saints Sergius and Bacchus, noted "friends" – watching over. The priest leads them in prayers that sound *very* much like wedding liturgy – there's talk of unity of souls, maybe a binding of hands with a stole, even a ceremonial kiss to seal the deal. At the end, they aren't pronounced "husband and husband," but rather "spiritual brothers." They walk out arm in arm, bonded for life in front of God and everybody. No rice throwing, but possibly some confused peasants wondering "Did we just witness a wedding or an adoption? Eh, pass the communion wine."

Officially, the Church maintained this was a chaste union, a bit like becoming blood brothers, elevated to a holy level. But come on – modern historians like the late John Boswell looked at the medieval liturgical texts and practically shouted, "If it walks like a duck and quacks like a duck…!" To Boswell, these ceremonies were basically same-sex marriages in disguise. Not all scholars agree (cue academic slap-fight with manuscripts as weapons), but the fact remains: the rite existed for centuries, and some of the paired-up brethren were almost certainly more than "bros."

There are actual recorded pairs who underwent adelphopoiesis. One famous example: Byzantine Emperor Basil I apparently entered such a brotherhood with a companion named John. Now, Basil also married (women) and did the usual emperor stuff, but the bond with John was evidently super important – they were buried together in the same tomb, which in those days was basically the equivalent of a joint Facebook account (you only do it if you're inseparable or one of you lost a bet). Another case from Western Europe: Sir William Neville and Sir John Clanvowe, two 14th-century English knights so tight-knit they took a vow of brotherhood, traveled everywhere together, and even died almost at the same time while on campaign abroad. They were buried side by side under a shared tombstone that had their family crests entwined like a heraldic hug. If that doesn't say "'til death do us part," what does? In their era, everyone just smiled and said "Oh, they're sworn brothers, how sweet." Today, we'd raise an eyebrow and say "Mm-hmm, *brothers*, sure."

The Church's stance nowadays is that adelphopoiesis was completely platonic – nothing to do with romance, nosiree. They liken it to, say, becoming god-brothers or a fraternity of two. And indeed, some pairs probably were just BFFs cementing their friendship legally and spiritually (especially useful for political alliances or inheritance purposes – a way to make your best bud into legal family so he can, for instance, inherit your estate). But given what we know about human nature… some of these pairings likely slid from "brotherhood" into "brotherhood with benefits." After all, if two men already felt a deep bond and perhaps attraction, what better cover than a Church-blessed partnership? Who's gonna question two "brothers" sharing a house or a bed? Move along, nothing sinful to see here – they're *brothers*, ok? (Wink.)

From a comedic standpoint, I love the idea that medieval clergy were basically offering a holy bromance ceremony. It's like those sitcom episodes where two straight friends pretend to be a gay couple to get some perk – except reverse that. Here, if anyone accused you of being lovers, you could indignantly reply, "Good heavens, no! We're *brothers* in Christ, shame on you for misinterpreting our very manly and completely chaste cohabitation!" Then go right back to making goo-goo eyes at each other once the nosy neighbor trots off.

Relationship wisdom from adelphopoiesis: If society gives you lemons, you slip through a loophole and make lemonade. These folks wanted a recognized union, and by Jove, they found one that the Church would rubber-stamp. It shows a kind of perseverance in love – not even the formidable medieval Church could prevent two determined souls from finding a way to be together, at least in spirit (and likely in flesh when curtains closed). For modern couples, the lesson is: there's always a way to formalize your commitment, even if you have to get creative. (Back when same-sex marriage was illegal, some couples made one partner legally adopt the other to get rights – how's that for a weird echo of "brother-making"?) Love truly laughs at absurd definitions.

Let's not forget the bosom buddies themselves. I like to imagine some of these couples-in-all-but-name living happily ever after, running a joint household, maybe even advising each other on which tunic looks best for Easter mass ("Brother, does this make me look portly?" – "Nay, brother, you are as handsome as Saint Michael." #MarriageGoals, medieval style). Possibly they had spats like any couple: who left the quill out uncapped? Did you spend too much from our joint purse at the tavern again? But unlike married hetero couples, they had the luxury of the world seeing nothing but two pious friends. In a twist of irony, by being less accepted, they might have dodged some scrutiny straight couples faced. No in-laws to nag them for grandkids, for instance!

Of course, not everyone was on board with Boswell's "gay wedding" theory of adelphopoiesis. Critics say, "No, no, it's about spiritual friendship only!" But even they must admit the romantic vibe in some of the rituals is palpable. I mean, one prayer in a Slavonic version of the rite literally beseeches God to grant the paired men "unfailing love in brotherhood" and compares their bond to that of famous inseparable duos from scripture. Substitute just a couple words, and you've got a Hallmark wedding vow. Whether the participants took *advantage* of that closeness later with some candlelit cuddles? That's between them, God, and maybe the confessional priest (who probably didn't hear a peep – after all, they weren't "sinning," they were just brothers... *wink*).

By now, we've toured quite the spectrum of medieval same-sex scenarios – secretive nuns, possibly smitten kings, openly racy poets, and ritualized male bonding. It's time to step back, take a breath of incense-tinged air, and address the big question: was the medieval world really as prudish and dark as people think when it comes to sexuality? Spoiler: nope. Let's debunk the myth with our final section.

Myth vs Reality – The "Dark Ages" weren't completely dark on sexuality. Official doctrine disapproved, but from Europe to the Middle East, same-sex love found ways to survive – in coded language, in poetry, in sworn brotherhoods.

The term "Dark Ages" often conjures images of a miserable, repressed time where everyone was dirty, nobody read books, and certainly no one was exploring the rainbow spectrum of love. But as we've seen through these tales, that's a bunch of medieval malarkey. Sure, the Middle Ages weren't exactly waving Pride flags (rainbows back then were mostly reserved for divine promises and unicorn decorations), yet same-sex love quietly but tenaciously threaded itself into the fabric of medieval life. Like ivy on a castle wall, it might have been tucked in the shadows, but it was definitely there.

Let's tackle the myth: "Everyone was straight, chaste, and dull until modern times." Ha! The reality is more interesting (and funnier). Medieval people were, first and foremost, people. They gossiped, they crushed on each other, they found ways to hook up or cohabit, even under the nose of authority. The human heart didn't suddenly start deviating from the hetero script in the 20th century – it's been ad-libbing all along.

Official doctrine, whether from the Church pulpit in Europe or the mosque minbar in the Middle East, largely condemned homosexual acts. That's true. We've got plenty of sermons, legal texts, and fire-and-brimstone warnings about the sin of sodomy, blah blah. But here's the kicker: preaching is one thing, practice is another. While a monk was busy denouncing "unnatural vice" on Sunday, on Monday Brother Lawrence might be penning a flowery note to Brother Hubert about last night's *intense prayer session* together (cough). Kingdoms had laws against gay sex, but enforcement was sporadic and often more about politics than piety. It's almost as if these societies collectively agreed to a "don't ask, don't tell (and if you do tell, speak in poetry)" policy.

From our journey:

- In that convent, same-sex love survived in coded letters. The nuns cloaked their passion in religious metaphor and natural imagery. Unless you knew what you were reading, one might think it's just overly affectionate platonic talk. But the two women involved knew the truth – and probably a few trusted confidantes did too. (I like to think at least one other nun was playing lookout or courier for them, giving a sly smile whenever a new letter was delivered.)

- At the royal courts, love survived in rumors and alliances. Maybe Richard and Philip truly had a thing, maybe not – but the very fact that rumor could exist means the concept was graspable. People had a framework for "men who are a bit too close," even if they joked about it in hushed tones. The idea of two men in love wasn't alien; it was just not publicly acknowledged. Kind of like Hollywood in the 1950s – everyone knew Rock Hudson had his "preferences," but it stayed off the record. Medieval courts similarly wink-winked and got on with business.

- In the Islamic world, love not only survived but thrived in poetry and song. You couldn't openly say "Hey, I'm into guys" on the street without potential trouble, but you could recite a beautiful ghazal about a beloved youth and earn nods of approval for your artistic talent. It's as if art was a safe zone where all desires could be expressed under cover of metaphor. (Pro tip: If you ever time-travel to the Abbasid court, maybe bring a sonnet or two up your sleeve; it apparently did wonders for acceptance.)

- Through adelphopoiesis, love survived in sworn brotherhoods blessed by the church. The brilliance of that strategy is how official and legitimate it was. It gave same-sex pairs a recognized status that commanded respect. The myth is medieval church = 100% homophobic villain; the reality is more nuanced. Some clergy surely suspected these "brothers" were more than friends, but as long as the appearances were kept up, it was live-and-let-live. After all, the Church cared about order and souls – if two people weren't causing a scandal and came to Mass, it was all good. (They might have to murmur an extra prayer of repentance if Saturday night got too rowdy, but hey.)

Were there tragedies? Undoubtedly, yes. We shouldn't paint the Middle Ages as a queer paradise – far from it. There were harsh punishments meted out at times, especially when politics or personal vendettas came into play. Accusing a rival of sodomy was a handy way to disgrace them. Some unlucky lovers got caught by the wrong people: the annals record monks punished for "relations," knights executed for allegedly seducing pages, etc. The Inquisition later on took a very dim view, to put it mildly. But those are the cases that make it into official records precisely because they were notable. For every one of those, we can imagine dozens of same-sex couples who flew under the radar, living their lives quietly, maybe always a bit on edge but finding moments of happiness in a hostile world.

So the reality is a patchwork: some darkness, yes, but also a lot of light in the cracks. Humanity's capacity for love and lust didn't press pause during the medieval era. Far from it – they had *fewer* outlets, so people got creative. They wrote secret poems in the margins of prayer books. They formed all-male (or all-female) communities where close bonds could develop without nosy outsiders. They used flowery "friendship" terms as a smoke screen for deeper relationships. They even leveraged the ambiguity of intense spiritual love – like how mystics would say they were "in love with God" but occasionally that fervor spilled over to a fellow monk or nun who just *embodied* the divine beauty for them (ahem, convenient).

In many ways, the Middle Ages had its own code, a queer coding if you will. Just as 20th-century gay men signaled with subtle fashion choices or references ("friend of Dorothy," anyone?), medieval same-sex inclined folks signaled with patron saints, poetry, and ceremonies. Saints Sergius and Bacchus (those legendary soldier-saints who were described in one text as "erastai" – lovers) became icons for brotherly devotion. The poetry of people like Abu Nuwas circulated and maybe gave a lonely teenager in Cairo hope that he wasn't alone in feeling that way. The existence of adelphopoiesis might have comforted two Byzantine guys that hey, we can actually legitimize our bond somewhat.

And what about the common folk? Surely not only nuns, kings, poets, and knights had all the fun. Indeed, we have less record of peasant Hank and Miller John shacking up – but it likely happened in villages, too. Perhaps they shrugged and called them lifelong bachelors who "share a cottage to save money." Perhaps two widow ladies decided to move in together for "companionship" and no one batted an eye because it was safer to assume it was just to ward off loneliness. The less status you had, sometimes the less scrutiny, ironically. Unless the local priest was a real hardliner, many communities probably practiced a form of quiet tolerance born of "mind your own business." After all, medieval life was tough enough; if your neighbor helped plow your field and paid his taxes, who cared what he did at night?

Myth debunked: The medieval world was not one giant heteronormative boot stamping out any deviation. It had its rules and punishments, yes, but also its rebels and romantics. The fact that we have love letters, poems, and even ecclesiastical rituals testifying to same-sex devotion means that even under strictures, love persevered. We see continuity of the human experience: those nuns could exchange letters just like modern lovers text. That's essentially the same impulse, only difference is the medium (and probably a lot more Latin). King Richard and King Philip's complicated relationship? Swap out chainmail for suits and you could have a modern political bromance scandal (the press conference would be *lit*). Abu Nuwas writing erotic poetry? He'd be a bestselling songwriter today, perhaps penning lyrics for Sam Smith. The brother-making ceremonies? Well, we finally got actual same-sex marriage in many countries – but it echoes that desire for formal recognition that existed long ago. History isn't a straight line (pun intended) – it's a tapestry with recurring patterns.

To wrap it up with a humorous bow (or maybe a medieval codpiece): The Middle Ages had its fair share of "Don't tell the pope" love stories. For every official decree saying "No, no, no," there were lovers whispering "yes, yes, yes" in secret. Was it risky? Sure. Was it done? Absolutely. And thank goodness, because it gives us these incredible, relatable stories. They're important, too, because they debunk the idea that LGBT history started with Oscar Wilde or Stonewall. Nope – it's been around as long as humanity, finding refuge in convents, castles, courts, and churches in creative ways.

Marriage lesson from all this big-picture stuff: Love is resilient. You can draft the harshest laws, shout from the highest pulpit, threaten fire and brimstone, yet somehow a love letter still gets written, a bed gets shared, a poem gets composed, a partnership gets blessed (albeit under a different name). And people will find humor, joy, and hope in their relationships despite the obstacles – just as we've found some humor and joy retelling their tales now. If medieval lovers could keep the flame alive in an era of dungeons and crusades, modern relationships should count themselves lucky (no plagues… well, scratch that, but at least Netflix and air conditioning!).

So the next time someone refers to the Middle Ages as benighted or sexually repressed, you have some stories to share – of nuns in love, kings in a cuddle, poetic rapture in Baghdad, and brothers by choice. The truth is, the medieval world was as complex and colorful as any other era, full of people who laughed, loved, and defied the odds. Monks, Moors, and medieval mysteries indeed – and perhaps not so mysterious after all, once you know where to look. In the grand saga of same-sex love through the ages, the Middle Ages chapters are as intriguing and instructive as any – proving that love truly is a timeless rogue, sneaking past barriers even in the unlikeliest of times. And that's a fact as fun as it is fascinating.

Chapter 6

Swashbucklers and Samurai – Early Modern Adventures in Same-Sex Love

History isn't all prim straight-laced marriages and "no homo" duels at dawn – in fact, some of the wildest love stories of the early modern world are as colorful and audacious as a summer blockbuster. We're talking sword-swinging samurai boyfriends, pirates who put the "mate" in "first mate," Native warriors shacking up with shamans, and even kings and queens flipping the script on royal romance. Buckle up (or rather, swashbuckle up) for a globe-trotting tour of same-sex love in the 16th and 17th centuries. It's witty, it's bold, it's occasionally scandalous – and it all goes to show that love and lust have always found a way, even when wearing a suit of armor or a pirate's eyepatch.

Way of the Warrior (and His Boyfriend)

Picture this: feudal Japan, 1600s. Two samurai stand under a blooming cherry blossom tree at sunset – one is a battle-hardened warrior in his prime, the other a fresh-faced teenage apprentice hanging on his every word. They're reciting poetry to each other about honor and devotion with just a hint of flirtation. No, this isn't the plot of a lost *Karate Kid* sequel or a niche anime romance – it's an actual samurai tradition known as wakashudō, the "way of youth." In a nutshell, samurai culture often encouraged an older warrior ("senpai," if you will) to mentor a younger male samurai-in-training, and their bond was part mentorship, part *passionate* romance. Think of it like a strict martial arts training montage, but set to a love ballad on the shakuhachi flute. Loyalty? Check. Sword skills? Check. A little side of forbidden love? Double-check – except it wasn't so forbidden back then!

Hard as it might be to imagine in our post-*Last Samurai* world, many Japanese warriors believed that the truest love was between men – specifically between an experienced samurai and his beloved pupil. They even worked it into their moral code. A warrior's vow to his male lover was considered as honorable as any vow could be. In fact, flipping through the literature and art of the time, you'd find that these warrior-to-warrior love stories were celebrated, idealized, even *expected*. Samurai would write tender haiku for their boyfriends before riding into battle. (Hallmark cards, eat your heart out.) Woodblock prints portrayed warrior couples embracing in between skirmishes. One could argue the fiercest weapon a samurai had – aside from a razor-sharp katana – was the devotion of his partner by his side.

Need a real historical example of this arms-and-heart alliance? Meet Oda Nobunaga, a warlord so legendary he's basically the Japanese equivalent of Darth Vader (minus the heavy breathing). Nobunaga had a teenaged page named Mori Ranmaru who was famed for his beauty, devotion, and let's be honest, *tush-kicking* loyalty. Ranmaru wasn't just fetching tea and sharpening swords – he was Nobunaga's probable lover. In 1582, when enemies ambushed Nobunaga, Ranmaru fought like a man possessed to protect his lord. Both tragically perished in the siege, presumably after exchanging one last tearful look in true dramatic fashion. It's said Ranmaru's loyalty unto death made him the MVP of samurai boyfriends. Their story was basically the 16th-century version of a tragic romance epic: think

Romeo and Romeo, with more swords and a higher body count. You can almost imagine the movie trailer voiceover: "In a world of war, one young samurai's love burned brighter than the temple flames at Honnō-ji."

What's wild to modern sensibilities is that back then this wasn't viewed as some scandal to be hushed up. Not at all! Samurai communities saw these relationships as win-win: the younger partner learned the ways of the warrior (and maybe some "pillow book" techniques on the side), and the older partner earned the youth's undying loyalty and affection. A well-known saying of the era suggested that *the bond between warrior lovers was stronger than the bond of marriage.* Who needs a wife to come home to when your battlefield bromance has your back through every arrow volley? In contrast to Europe's pearl-clutching prudery of the time, Japan's samurai clans were more like, "Two men in love? As long as you both can swing a sword, we're cool with it." Some daimyōs (feudal lords) even encouraged their vassals to pair off with a comrade for morale's sake. Leave it to the samurai to turn "unit cohesion" into an art form – literally.

Now, don't get the wrong idea that it was all serious ritual and no fun. These warrior boyfriends could be playful too. They often spent off-duty hours composing love poems or sneaking off to hot springs together, probably making up cheesy pickup lines like, "Your eyes shine brighter than my *katana* blade, my love." Samurai society winked and nodded because they believed such love made the men braver. (After all, who wouldn't fight like hell if your sweetheart was watching from the castle ramparts?) It's basically the original *"fight for the one you love"* trope.

Modern pop culture sadly hasn't given this tradition its due. (Hello, Hollywood – where's our sweeping samurai love story?) Remember how *Star Wars* had the whole Jedi-master and padawan thing? Imagine if Obi-Wan and Anakin's bond had been, well, a little more personal – maybe the galaxy's problems would have been solved with a lot less angst and missing limbs. Or consider if Mr. Miyagi's karate lessons to Daniel in *The Karate Kid* came with romantic subtext – that crane kick training would have gotten *awkwardly* intimate. The point is, real history served us an unexpected twist: the "way of the warrior" included being a lover and fighter all at once.

Marriage Lesson (Samurai Edition): A relationship built on mutual respect and loyalty can be literally life-saving. The samurai teach us that couples who train together, slay together (sometimes *literally* slay) have unbreakable bonds. And hey, maybe the key to a lasting relationship is treating your partner like your trusted sword – keep 'em sharp, handle with care, and never let them rust. Just maybe skip the part where you both choose seppuku over separation – that's a bit *too* dramatic for modern romance.

As the sun sets on our samurai sweethearts exchanging love poems under the cherry blossoms, we now turn our spyglass to the horizon. Beyond the seas, another breed of fearless lovers was making waves – quite literally. Hoist the rainbow Jolly Roger and prepare to set sail for the Caribbean, where swashbuckling pirates were proving that "X marks the spot" could also mean the spot where two mateys tied the knot...

Pirate "Mateys" for Life

Meanwhile, on the high seas of the 1600s, pirates were busy redefining "Ahoy, matey!" into something a lot more domestic. Picture a creaky deck under the tropical sun, two burly buccaneers clinking their rum-filled tankards, gazing into each other's one good eye with affection. (Cue the ocean breeze and perhaps a thoughtful parrot squawking "I do.") In the lawless paradise of Tortuga and across the Caribbean, swarthy pirates weren't just plundering Spanish galleons – some were also walking down an imaginary aisle in what amounted to pirate civil unions. They called it matelotage (from the French word *matelot* for "sailor" or "pal"). In plain English, matelotage was basically "matey-marriage." Two male pirates would pledge to share their loot, watch each other's backs in battle, and basically be each other's ride-or-die. In a world with no health insurance or 401(k)s, your pirate-partner *was* your benefits package – plus a snuggle on a cold sea night. And it wasn't a one-in-a-thousand fluke: in rough-and-tumble pirate havens, these same-sex partnerships were about as routine as the daily ration of rum.

To be fair, pirates were equal opportunity plunderers *and* lovers – some matelotage unions might have been more "no homo (but all the bromance)" for practical mutual benefit, while others were full-on love stories with added oomph behind the cannon fire. Life on a pirate ship was harsh: danger at every turn, scurvy looming if you skipped your citrus, and a serious lack of ladies on board. The solution for many? Buddy up with your best pirate bro and make him your "sea spouse." Why pine for a wife back in Port Royal when you could have a partner in crime right there in the crow's nest? These pirate pairs shared everything – booty (yes, even *that* kind of booty, wink wink), bounty, and bed. If one of them fell in battle or got an unlucky bout of yellow fever, the other would inherit their treasure chest, just like a next of kin. It's oddly wholesome: a makeshift life insurance policy wrapped in a romance, under the black flag.

In fact, let's raise a tankard to the Pirate Partnership Code – if we wrote it out, it might have gone something like this:

- **Share All Booty:** *Treasure, loot, doubloons – and yes, perhaps even the "booty" in the cheeky sense – everything is split down the middle. You steal a Spanish gold chain? It's going around both our necks (aww, matching necklaces!).*

- **Have Each Other's Backs (Literally):** *In battle, your matelot is your #1. You fight through back-to-back like an unstoppable* **pirate power couple,** *each ready to shoot or stab anyone who threatens your beloved. Talk about relationship goals.*

- **No Pirate Left Behind:** *If one is marooned, the other shares his rations. If one loses a hand (hey, hooks are in this season), the other is there to fasten the straps. Sickness, injury, or a particularly nasty hangover – you nurse each other through it.*

- **Inheritance Clause:** *Should ye tragically meet Davy Jones's Locker, your partner gets your share of the loot. (This one caused more than a few greedy* **in-law spats** *when actual wives back home discovered they'd been cut out in favor of First Mate Fabio.)*

- **Rum and Relaxation:** *Every night, you split a bottle of rum and regale each other with tales of daring. Who needs a honeymoon when you have a nightly* **grog date** *under the stars?*

Now, before we get too sentimental, let's acknowledge pirates were still pirates – rough around the edges with a flair for the profane. But that doesn't mean their same-sex unions were any less meaningful. In fact, colonial governors and clergy were *horrified* by matelotage. The authorities clutched their pearls (or crucifixes) at reports of pirates forming "unnatural" liaisons. One infamous French governor of Tortuga was so freaked out by all the male-male canoodling among his buccaneers that in 1645 he literally begged France to send over 2,000 prostitutes to the island, hoping an influx of available women would straighten out (pun intended) the boys. We can almost hear his panicked plea: "Mon Dieu, these pirates are marrying each other! Quick, send ladies – lots of ladies!" Spoiler: a boatload of courtesans did arrive, but it's safe to say old habits die hard on the high seas. The pirates found room in their hearts for the ladies *and* their matelots, or they politely said, "Thanks, but no thanks, we're kind of spoken for."

Pop culture often paints pirates as rum-soaked, womanizing scallywags (looking at you, Captain Jack Sparrow). But the reality is more diverse and frankly more fabulous. It's almost like a queer *Pirates of the Caribbean* spinoff was playing out in real history. (In fact, a recent TV show *Our Flag Means Death* had the right idea, depicting pirates in… let's say *intimate* friendships.) Imagine if *Pirates of the Caribbean* had dared to show Jack Sparrow and Will Turner exchanging vows on the deck of the Black Pearl, sharing not just the compass but also a mortgage on their Nassau beach house. That would actually be closer to what some pirate crews lived. Sure, they didn't have an official priest or a "By the power vested in me by the Pirate Code…" ceremony (although *that* scene would've been gold), but they had each other – and in a violent, uncertain world, that's the treasure that truly mattered.

Let's also not pretend these pirate partnerships were entirely chaste "just bros being bros." Plenty of contemporary observers quietly noted the *affectionate* aspects. (Translation: the pirates were definitely getting it on when off duty.) The Spanish Inquisition would have combusted on the spot had they tried to police Captain Blackbeard's cabin after hours. But out on the open ocean, far from the rule of church and state, a pair of pirates could carve out a life together by their own rules. It's rebellious, it's romantic, it's a bit salty – basically the perfect recipe for a great sea shanty.

Marriage Lesson (Pirate Edition): Find yourself a partner who will share their booty with you – finances and feelings alike. Partnership is about having each other's backs through stormy weather and fierce battles. And communication is key: if you can draw up an agreement on how to split stolen treasure and survive life-threatening adventures together, you can probably handle doing the dishes and paying bills on time. Also, a little pirate role-play never hurts to keep the spark alive… aye aye, Captain!

We've now navigated from the disciplined romance of the samurai to the rambunctious unions of pirates. But our voyage through early modern same-sex love isn't over. Steer your compass toward the New World, where conquistadors stumbled upon something that really blew their mind – and it wasn't El Dorado. It was the sight of brave indigenous warriors settling down with male spouses, a cultural curveball that left those armored explorers more dazed than if they'd been whacked with a tomahawk…

Two-Spirit Tribes

When Spanish conquistadors marched into the Americas in the 1500s, they expected gold, glory, maybe the occasional human-sacrifice scare. What they didn't expect was to find villages where a respectable warrior could be hitched to another man – and nobody in the village batted an eye. To the buttoned-up Catholic sensibilities of Europe, this was the equivalent of an alien abduction. One flabbergasted Spaniard in 1542 sputtered about witnessing *"one devilish thing... a man married to another man."* You can almost see him writing that in a letter home, his quill quivering with shock as if he'd just seen the actual devil doing the tango. This befuddled explorer was Álvar Núñez Cabeza de Vaca, and in his account of roaming around what's now the American Southwest, he basically clutched his rosary and described how some indigenous men lived as women and even took husbands. The poor guy was so scandalized you'd think he walked in on his parents at an *Eyes Wide Shut* party.

So, what was really going on? Were these just isolated instances of "oops, didn't understand what I saw"? Not at all. In many Native American cultures, there existed (and still exist) people we today call Two-Spirit individuals – people who embody both male and female qualities, often taking on roles or clothing of the opposite (or another) gender. They weren't seen as freaks or "sinners" by their own people, but rather as a natural and sometimes even sacred part of the community. Many tribes believed a person who was Two-Spirit had special spiritual powers or deeper insight, kind of like having an extra vibe with the spirit world. And guess what? These individuals could and did marry members of the same sex (from a European viewpoint), often in every way that *hetero* couples would – except perhaps with more interesting wardrobe choices. For example, a Two-Spirit person born male might live as a woman and marry a man (making the Spaniards' heads explode), functioning as a wife in the tribe's eyes. Or a warrior might take a Two-Spirit person as his spouse, appreciating that they occupied a revered, feminine role. Far from being stigmatized, some of these unions were honored as bringing balance or blessings – a far cry from the "hellfire and damnation" reaction of our Iberian invaders.

Let's set a scene: A Spanish soldier named, say, Hernando, is trudging through a village after a long day's conquest, looking for some corn and a place to crash. He sees a household with two "men" cohabitating. One of them is dressed in women's attire, grinding maize and gossiping with the other ladies, while her husband (who's biologically male) is out hunting or preparing for war. Hernando does a double-take, rubs his eyes, maybe mutters "¿Qué carajo...?" under his breath. He inquires and finds out; indeed, they are considered a married couple locally. The neighbors aren't scandalized – in fact, they might have been at the wedding, eating maize cakes and wishing the couple well. Mind = blown for poor Hernando. Back home, the Spanish Inquisition would be snapping on the rubber gloves (or the 16th-century equivalent) to deal with this "heresy." But here in the New World, it's just another Tuesday. One can imagine his letter to the Spanish governor: *"Your Excellency, you won't believe this. These natives have men living as women who marry other men! One even offered to set me up with his son – I nearly fainted into the campfire."*

The conquistadors, unsurprisingly, labeled this a monstrous sin. The phrase "one devilish thing" from Cabeza de Vaca's account shows how they framed it as diabolical. They probably went to confession immediately, whispering, "Forgive me Father, for I have seen fabulous things I cannot un-see." Some even took violent action – we have tragic records of Spanish and later European colonizers punishing or executing Two-Spirit individuals to enforce their own moral code. (So much for "New World," same old intolerance.) It's a dark footnote that amid all the humorous culture clash, there were real human costs.

Yet, despite persecution, the tradition of Two-Spirit people endured through the centuries in many tribes, quietly resisting eradication. Many Native communities recognized up to five genders in their societies – talk about being ahead of the curve! Europe was barely coping with two (and largely failing at that, let's be honest), while some indigenous Americans were like, "Gender? Oh, we've got a whole spectrum, honey. Catch up." Two-Spirits often served as healers, matchmakers, or warriors themselves. In some tribes, a man might actually prefer a Two-Spirit spouse because they were seen as especially wise or skilled partners. So while Spanish hombres were busy writing "OMG this is so evil!" in their diaries, the tribes were getting on with life, love, and possibly giving a side-eye like, "We've been doing this forever, why you acting brand new?"

From our modern standpoint, it's heartening and a bit ironic: the so-called "savages" turned out to be more accepting of diverse love and gender expression than the supposedly civilized Europeans. If there's a pop culture analogy, it's like those teen movies where the uptight parents (the Spaniards) freak out about the kids throwing a drag party, but the kids (the indigenous folks) are just expressing themselves freely. We know who history *should* label as the enlightened ones in that scenario!

Marriage Lesson (Two-Spirit Edition): Love is love, but context is everything. What one culture calls "devilish" might be another culture's cherished tradition. When it comes to relationships, don't let outside prejudices dictate what's right. Be like the Two-Spirit couples – live your truth proudly, love who you love, and maybe keep a humorous diary in case some nosy conquistador stumbles into your village. Also, if your relatives don't understand your marriage? Just remind them that at least you didn't make a Spanish priest perform an exorcism at your wedding – so really, it could be worse.

Having seen the New World's version of "Modern Family: 16th Century Edition," let's hop back across the Atlantic. Europe may have been less publicly accepting, but that doesn't mean same-sex love wasn't happening behind those castle walls. In fact, one of the biggest trendsetters of the age – a king famous enough to get a Bible named after him – was gayer than a rainbow doublet. Time to meet a British monarch who treated his male favorite like a royal hubby, centuries before Netflix made royal dramas cool...

King James's Favorite "Queen"

The year is 1615 in England. King James I swaggers about the royal court with a mischievous grin. By his side is a dashing young noble, George Villiers – freshly appointed as the Duke of Buckingham and even more freshly appointed as the King's *everything*. James is absolutely smitten. Picture an infatuated sugar daddy with a crown, and you've got the vibe. Gossip flies through the court quicker than a carrier pigeon on espresso: "Have you seen how the King looks at Buckingham?!" Ladies of the court fan themselves in shock (or is it envy?). Courtiers raise eyebrows so high they hit their powdered wigs. The Queen (James's wife, Anne of Denmark) probably rolls her eyes and focuses on her embroidery. Because James – the guy commissioning the King James Bible and ruling over Shakespeare's England – is openly doting on Buckingham like he's the fairest of them all.

How open, you ask? Let's just say if Snapchat existed in the 1600s, James would have had a custom filter with George's face surrounded by heart emojis. The king wrote Buckingham passionate letters that make modern love texts look tame. In one letter, James literally signed off as "your dear dad and husband", calling Buckingham "my sweet child and wife." (Yes, you read that correctly. King *James*, a grown man in his 50s, calling himself hubby and dad to a 20-something duke – if that's not a kink, it's certainly a very specific role-play.) Buckingham, for his part, wasn't shy about reciprocating affection, though his letters are unfortunately harder to come by (perhaps he was wisely cautious or just busy enjoying the royal favor). The king also gave his favorite pet names; he called George "Steenie," supposedly because young Villiers had a face as angelic as Saint Stephen in a painting. Imagine being so cute the king names you after a saint – talk about #Blessed.

Their correspondence reads like something straight out of a historical romance novel with the names barely changed. James cooed that he would rather be banished from his kingdom than live "a sorrowful widow's life" without George. Essentially, "If you leave me, I'll die, love – xoxo, Your King." He even pulled a biblical parallel once, telling his shocked advisors, *"Christ had his John, and I have my George."* (Cue collective gasps from the pious peanut gallery. James basically compared himself to Jesus – and Buckingham to the "Beloved Disciple" John. As pickup lines go, that's one way to justify your male lover to a bunch of bishops: *Hey, if Jesus could have a favorite guy, so can I.* Bold move, Jimmy.)

Public displays of affection? Oh, there were displays. James, famously not the most subtle man at court, would cuddle and kiss Buckingham in front of other nobles. One observer from France scandalously remarked that the King of England "caresses that duke in front of everyone, as if he were his mistress." Imagine a royal banquet: platters of roasted swan being served, violinists playing Baroque music, and in the middle of it King James is basically giving Buckingham a shoulder rub and googly eyes. If Twitter existed, #JamesAndGeorge would be trending along with memes of "King James Version 2.0: Now with more romance." It's no wonder the *rumor mill* of the time went into overdrive. Some critics tried to downplay it ("It's just a *very close friendship*, uh-huh, sure"), but many knew exactly what was up – a saucy poem even circulated that bluntly put it: *"The King of England*...** does what with the Duke of Buckingham?"* (Let's just say the blank is a four-letter word that rhymes with "bucks." Subtle, those 17th-century poets.)

Despite the whispers and raised eyebrows, James didn't really care. He was the king, after all. Who was going to tell him to dial down the rainbow romance? He loaded Buckingham with titles, lands, money – the whole nine yards. George Villiers went from a minor country gentleman to Earl, then Marquess, then Duke, basically speedrunning the aristocratic ladder thanks to the king's love (and perhaps other skills we won't speculate on). Other nobles seethed with jealousy – imagine being a hard-working courtier for years, and this pretty young lad waltzes in and monopolizes the royal heart. It's the classic tale: middle-aged powerful man falls for hot younger newcomer, and everyone else has to grin and bear it. One politician at the time, grumbling about Buckingham's hold on the king, coined the phrase "the favorite" to describe George – and that term has stuck in history for royal paramours who aren't officially spouses.

Let's sprinkle in some modern analogy: It's as if the President decided to publicly canoodle with his handsome intern and then made that intern the Secretary of State and head of the Treasury for good measure. Scandal much? And yet, James managed to mostly get away with it. Sure, the Puritans were outraged (but they were always outraged about something; it's their hobby). Foreign ambassadors tattled in letters to their kings about the "immoral" English court. But James? He sat on his throne, likely *snuggling* up next to Buckingham during long coach rides and whispering sweet state secrets in his ear, utterly unbothered.

Did it ever backfire? Not in James's lifetime. Buckingham remained his one and only (at least in James's heart) until the king's death. After James died, Buckingham actually got into a pickle – he wasn't as beloved by James's heir, Charles I, and eventually some disgruntled folks assassinated Buckingham (occupational hazard of being a royal favorite with too much power). But the love between James and George left an undeniable mark on history. King James I, the guy whose name graces the most famous English Bible, is also a prominent figure in LGBTQ history, whether the church folks like it or not. You could say he put the "King" in "kinky" by effectively making a man his queen consort in all but name.

And let's give a shout-out to Queen Anne, James's actual wife. To her credit, she didn't stir up drama about the royal love triangle – perhaps she had her own thing going or just figured it was politically wiser to let sleeping dukes lie. Maybe she and James had an arrangement, or maybe she just thought "thank goodness he's leaving me alone, now I can read books in peace." In any case, James and Buckingham had something special, bizarre, and surprisingly transparent for its time.

Marriage Lesson (Royal Edition): If a king in the 1600s could openly write love letters to his boyfriend and call him "wife," then surely we can all be a bit bolder in expressing affection. Be proud of your love, and don't shy away from a cutesy pet name or two (perhaps skip "child" – that one doesn't translate well to modern ears). Also, power imbalance in relationships – we *saw* how James showered George with promotions. For us regular folks, that might equate to hogging the TV remote or deciding all the vacation plans. Take a lesson from James: love thrives better when you treat your partner as an equal (or in his case, practically a demigod). Finally, maybe hide the gushy letters in a safe place… unless you want them quoted centuries later for everyone's amusement!

> *From a king who practically shouted his same-sex devotion from the rooftops (or castle turrets), we now turn to a queen who took a different route – by swearing off marriage entirely and donning men's clothing. If King James was the "husband" in his royal romance, our next leading lady was having none of that hetero matrimonial nonsense. Pack your bags for the frosty north of Europe, where a crown-wearing rebel named Christina decided being a queen was fine – but being a wife? Hard pass…*

Queens in Drag

Queen Christina of Sweden might just be one of the greatest gender-bending, expectation-defying divas of the 17th century. Think of her as a cross between *Mulan* and *Prince* – a woman who wore men's clothes, balked at the idea of marrying a dude, and basically said, "You know what, keep your throne, I'm outta here" when the pressure got too real. Let's set the scene: It's the 1640s in Stockholm. Young Christina, officially *King* (yes, King – her dad insisted she be titled as such) of Sweden, is supposed to be the perfect princess-turned-queen. Find a nice prince, make royal babies, secure the dynasty – you know the drill. Christina, however, had other ideas. She enjoyed scholarly debates, horseback riding, hunting, and collecting art. She wore pants (gasp!), skipped the fancy gowns whenever she could, and even *horrified* foreign ambassadors by showing up to formal events dressed in a chic military-style outfit rather than an elegant dress. One report noted she walked like a man, sat and talked like a man, basically gave zero damns about acting "ladylike." In a century where women in pants were about as common as smartphones at a Mennonite church, Christina was making a statement with every stride in her boots.

Now, the biggest royal duty of any monarch, especially a queen, was to get married and pop out heirs. Suitors lined up for Christina's hand – kings, princes, dukes, you name it. She gave them all the cold shoulder. In fact, she spoke about marriage with absolute disgust. Our girl dropped some epic one-liners that could be lyrics in a punk rock song. Case in point: "I cannot bear to be *used by a man* the way a peasant uses his fields," she once said. (OH SNAP! That's 17th-century for "Keep your hands off my body, you filthy men, I'm not your property.") She even prayed to God to change her aversion to marriage, but alas (or thankfully), nothing changed – she was just not into dudes that way, period. In one poignant statement, Christina declared, "It is impossible for me to marry. My character is simply not suited to marriage." Now, given the times, she phrased it like a personal quirk, but reading between the lines: this queen preferred her own company – or the company of women – over any princely consort.

And indeed, Christina had her favorites too, just not the kind that would ever put a baby in her. Enter Countess Ebba Sparre, a lady-in-waiting at court and the apple of Christina's eye. Christina nicknamed her "Belle" (French for "beautiful," because why be subtle when you're a queen?). The two women were inseparable. They wrote gushy letters when apart – one surviving letter from Christina reads like a 17th-century lesbian love text: "I greet you a million times, kissing your hands" and lamenting how she can never be truly happy without seeing her dear Belle. Back at court, they spent *loads* of time together, often sharing a bed during overnight journeys or stays. (Travel tip: always bring your favorite lady to cuddle on long carriage rides through cold Swedish nights.) The ladies of the court surely whispered behind their fans about the Queen and the Countess's "special friendship," but who was going to tell the monarch to knock it off? Christina basically ran one of the earliest documented "Don't ask, don't tell (because it's obvious anyway)" scenarios in royal history.

Christina's closeness to women and her utter disinterest in any man (she even called one of her hapless suitors, the King of Denmark, an *"idiot"* to his face when he tried to woo her – ouch) has cemented her status as a bit of a queer icon avant la lettre. Some modern scholars debate her exact orientation or identity – was she a lesbian? Bisexual? Trans masc? The terminology doesn't neatly apply, but one thing's clear: she wasn't playing by 17th-century hetero rules. And society's expectations? She tossed those out like last season's fashion. She famously eschewed traditionally feminine habits; gossip at the time sniped that she refused to comb her hair (teenage rebellion level:

expert) and would wear the same unfussy outfit days in a row – something unthinkable for a queen of that era. Basically, she was punk rock 300 years before punk existed.

All this came to a head in 1654. Rather than let her ministers strong-arm her into a political marriage and turning her into a broodmare for the next king, Christina did the unthinkable: she abdicated her throne. That's right, she broke up with an entire kingdom. In a grand ceremony, she took off her crown, swapped her royal regalia for a simple travel outfit (probably pants, of course), and handed over power to her bewildered cousin. It was the 17th-century equivalent of quitting your high-paying job to go live your best life on a beach somewhere – except in her case it was converting to Catholicism and moving to Rome, but hey, same energy. Europe was stunned. A queen had voluntarily given up power and wealth *because she didn't want to get married* (and because she wanted religious freedom to be Catholic – but let's face it, the marriage thing was a huge factor). Pamphlets and papers across the continent buzzed with speculation: "Was she secretly a man? Was she in love with a woman? Is she mad?!" The patriarchy's collective brain short-circuited trying to comprehend a woman who valued her personal autonomy over, you know, running a country.

Once free of Swedish expectations, Christina never did marry (told ya so!). Instead, she lived as a kind of eccentric intellectual in Rome – wearing men's attire more frequently, socializing with artists, philosophers, and cardinals, and presumably flirting with any intriguing ladies she pleased. She even set up a theatre and was rumored to enjoy watching *ballet* with handsome male dancers... there were whispers she had a dalliance or two with men in her later years, just to complicate the narrative, but if so it seems she regarded men as occasional amusements rather than lifelong partners. The core truth remained: she refused to be tied down, in any sense. When she died, she had "never been owned by any man," which, for her era, is as radical as it gets.

Christina's story has been told in film and literature – most famously, Greta Garbo portrayed her in the 1933 movie *Queen Christina*, adding a Hollywood wink to the idea she might have loved her lady-in-waiting. Modern audiences view her as an early example of women defying the binary expectations of gender and sexuality. If we were to drop a pop culture analogy, she's a bit like a 1600s version of a *rockstar princess who burns out of the royal life to live authentically.* Imagine Princess Leia saying "Screw the Rebellion, I'm gonna do me," or Disney's Elsa singing "Let It Go" not about ice powers but about ditching heteronormativity and running off into the sunset with her best gal pal. Christina's life was that bold.

Marriage Lesson (Runaway Queen Edition): Stay true to yourself, even if it means defying everyone's expectations. Marriage isn't for everyone, and that's okay – better to abdicate the altar than say "I do" for the wrong reasons. If a queen can upend her entire life to avoid marrying the wrong person (or any person), you can certainly survive the side-eye from Aunt Mildred when you tell her you're not settling for anything less than the real deal (or that you're not settling at all). Also, wardrobe is personal – wear whatever makes you feel royally yourself, be it a gown, a tuxedo, or a comfy pair of yoga pants. Confidence is the best crown.

From samurai lovers dying with honor, to pirate partners swearing oaths on the high seas; from Native Two-Spirit unions that shocked conquistadors, to kings and queens breaking the rules of romance – the early modern world was far more fabulous and diverse than most history books let on. Same-sex love has always found a way, in the unlikeliest of places and often in defiance of the era's norms. These tales aren't just juicy gossip from days of yore; they carry the echoes of a truth still relevant today: love is a rebellious force. It laughs at laws, thumbs its nose at convention, and flourishes in the hearts of the bold. So the next time someone says "traditional marriage," remind them that tradition itself is a wild tapestry – one that very much includes swashbucklers and samurai, pirates and princes, shamans and queens, all writing their own love stories long before hashtags and headlines. History, it turns out, was *always* rainbow-colored – you just needed to know where to look. And that, dear reader, is a fact as fun as it is fascinating.

Chapter 7

Wigs and Wit – 18th Century Enlightenment (and Entrapments)

Ladies of Llangollen – Two Irish women, Lady Eleanor Butler and Sarah Ponsonby, eloped in 1778 and lived together for 50 years; their 'romantic friendship' defied expectations.

Lady Eleanor Butler and Sarah Ponsonby were two Irish women who looked at 18th-century society's plan for them – marriage to some dull gentleman – and said, "No, thanks, we'll make our own happily ever after." In 1778, they carried out a daring midnight elopement together. Disguised in men's clothing and armed with a pistol (and a little dog named Frisk), they escaped their families' homes and fled to Wales. After a bit of drama (their first escape was foiled by outraged relatives, but they eventually won their freedom), the pair settled in a cozy cottage in Llangollen, Wales, determined to live life on their own terms. Think of it as an 18th-century blueprint for the ultimate alternative lifestyle: two well-bred ladies setting up house together, no husbands in sight, with a faithful maid to help out and nobody to tell them how to behave.

In their self-described "delightful retirement" at Plas Newydd (their new home's name), Eleanor and Sarah spent the next fifty years in devoted companionship. They read books to each other, tended a lovely garden, took long walks in matching riding habits, and basically lived the original #cottagecore lesbian dream. At a time when women of their class were expected to be ballroom belles or baby-making machines, these two chose a different adventure – one filled with quiet domestic bliss and intellectual partnership. They became known far and wide as the "Ladies of Llangollen," and their little love nest turned into a curious tourist attraction for high society. Poets, aristocrats, even royalty dropped by to meet them and see this extraordinary household. Visitors were charmed by the ladies' wit, learning, and hospitality. Many probably left scratching their heads, wondering if these "romantic friends" were something more. (Spoiler alert: all signs point to yes.)

Polite society didn't have the vocabulary to call Eleanor and Sarah a married couple, but that's essentially what they were. They shared a bed and a life, called each other endearments like "my beloved," and stood by each other through every challenge for half a century. People whispered that they were eccentric, but mostly they were respected – perhaps because the idea of two gentlewomen in love was too far outside the 18th-century norm to even conceive. The Ladies themselves never openly addressed the nature of their relationship (doing so would have been unthinkable then), but they didn't need to. They had carved out a safe haven for their love in a world that had no rulebook for them. Over time they became symbols of enduring same-sex devotion – proof that two women could create a happy, meaningful life together despite all societal expectations.

Marriage lesson? Eleanor and Sarah teach us that a successful partnership is one you define for yourselves. Sometimes the recipe for lasting love is as simple as this: find someone who will run away with you, build a cozy home, and grow old by your side – critics and conventions be damned. Their story is a timeless reminder that true love might not fit the mold, but it can flourish brilliantly in its own little garden of Eden.

Molly Houses & Macaronis – Georgian London's gay subculture included underground clubs, same-sex 'weddings,' and flamboyant elite macaronis (think 1700s drag brunch).

In Georgian London, beneath the powdered wigs and prim manners, there thrived a secret gay nightlife. Clandestine meeting places known as "molly houses" were the 18th-century equivalent of underground gay bars. By day they might be unassuming taverns or coffeehouses; by night they transformed into safe havens where men who loved men could be themselves. Inside, the atmosphere was warm, bawdy, and defiantly free. Men adopted playful female aliases and sometimes even cross-dressed in ladies' attire; they danced together, and even held mock weddings. Picture a candlelit back room where two grooms exchange vows and maybe a daring kiss, while friends cheer quietly. These ceremonies weren't legal (far from it), but the sentiment was real – a bold declaration of love in a world that forbade it. It was like a secret drag ball. The courage and community found in those back rooms were both heartwarming and dangerous.

Dangerous, because outside those walls the law was lying in wait. Periodically, moral crusaders and city watchmen would raid molly houses, dragging men out to face harsh justice. In 18th-century London, a secret knock at the door wasn't just for style – it was for survival. Men caught in these raids could be charged with sodomy (a capital crime) or the catch-all "sodomitical assault." Punishments were brutal: some men were hanged, others chained in the pillory and pelted by mobs. The threat of ruin or death hung over every romantic rendezvous. The contrast was stark: inside a molly house you might find laughter, acceptance, and a makeshift family; outside, the slightest slip could mean public humiliation or worse. Enlightenment or not, the establishment was intent on snuffing out what it saw as deviance. The molly subculture had to stay clever and cautious – it was literally love (and fun) in the time of peril.

Meanwhile, in the very same city, up on the gleaming streets of the West End, another phenomenon was turning heads – the Macaronis. These were elite young fashionistas whose motto might as well have been "more is more." Fresh from their Grand Tours in Italy, they came home obsessed with extravagant foreign fashions. A Macaroni would strut around with a ridiculously tall wig, a tiny hat perched jauntily on top, and lavish silks and lace covering his body – every inch adorned to impress. Think of them as the 1770s equivalent of flamboyant influencers – the kind who made old-school folks mutter into their tea, "Good heavens, that fellow looks positively absurd." Many a satirical cartoon showed Macaronis as gender-bending peacocks. (The very term "macaroni" became slang for a dandy who was too fashionable for his own good.) Not all of these gents were gay, mind you, but they definitely stretched the boundaries of 18th-century masculinity. In an era when men were supposed to be plain and stoic, the Macaronis blazed a trail of flamboyant self-expression – strutting right over gender norms in their high heels.

The coexistence of molly houses and Macaronis in Georgian society highlights a juicy double standard. Working-class gay men had to hide in shadowy taverns, literally risking their necks for a dance or a kiss. Meanwhile, an aristocratic dandy could mince down Pall Mall in makeup and satin – and though people might snicker or sneer, he'd usually stroll off unscathed as long as he was well-connected. The elite enjoyed a certain immunity behind their wealth and status, whereas the lower classes bore the brunt of the era's homophobic laws. Still, both groups were, each in their own way, challenging the norms of their time. One did it in secret, creating a vibrant underground world of their own. The other did it in broad daylight with feathers, frills, and a fanfare of scandalous style. Together, they proved that no matter how rigid society's rules, people will find a way to live and love authentically – whether in hidden corners or in outrageous costumes on city streets.

Marriage lesson? From the molly houses we learn that love will create its own rituals and sanctuaries even when it's pushed underground. A commitment ceremony in a dingy tavern can be as heartfelt as any church wedding when it's all you've got. And from the Macaronis we learn the power of unapologetic authenticity – sometimes you have to flaunt who you are and let the world adjust (or gossip) as it will. In any marriage or partnership, being true to yourself and supportive of your partner's true self is key. If two grooms in 1770 could pledge their hearts in a candlelit backroom while wearing wigs and petticoats, we can surely be a little braver about living and loving on our own terms today.

Pirate Queens of the Caribbean – Anne Bonny and Mary Read dressed as men, sailed as pirates, and may have been romantically involved – history meets Hollywood fantasy.

Yo-ho, yo-ho, a pirate's life for… two? Meet Anne Bonny and Mary Read, the fearsome female duo of the early 1700s Caribbean. These pirate queens broke every rule in the book. Each of them was already masquerading as a man to live the pirate life (disguises were the only ticket into the buccaneer boys' club). When they wound up on the same ship – captained by Anne's lover, the roguish Calico Jack Rackham – destiny (and drama) took the wheel. Anne initially thought Mary was just a dashing young fellow and reportedly developed a crush on "him." Imagine her surprise (and perhaps secret delight) when Mary privately confessed, "Um, actually, I'm a woman too." Cue the jaw drop! Instead of rivals, they became instant confidantes, bonded by the enormous secret they shared. Two women among unruly men, they watched each other's backs and, according to later legend, maybe stole a few affectionate moments below deck. It's easy to picture them at midnight on the quiet ship, sharing whispered stories of how they ended up there – perhaps even realizing that in each other they'd found someone who truly understood.

Their bravery was the stuff of legend. In one battle, Anne and Mary fought side by side, pistols firing and cutlasses swinging, while many of their male crewmates hid below in a drunken stupor. (Mary allegedly shouted at the useless lot to come up and fight "like men" – a hilarious rebuke coming from a woman in men's clothing.) These ladies could out-swear, out-drink, and out-fight most of their crew, all while keeping their true identities under wraps. They were, quite frankly, action heroes ahead of their time – think of them as a gritty Pirates of the Caribbean duo, but with a provocative twist that Hollywood has yet to fully embrace.

Eventually, the law caught up with Calico Jack's company. In 1720, Anne, Mary and the rest of the crew were captured by the English navy. Jack and the other men were quickly tried and sentenced to hang. Anne and Mary, however, pulled a clever last-minute gambit: they "pleaded the belly," claiming to be pregnant. Under 18th-century law, pregnant women could have their executions delayed (and often commuted), since no one wanted to hang an unborn child. The court bought it, postponing their sentences. As the story goes, Mary did indeed seem to be expecting – but she fell ill in prison and died before she could give birth (if there was a baby at all). Anne's fate after that is a bit of a mystery. One tale says her wealthy father pulled some strings and brought her back home to start a new life under an assumed name. Another whispers that she escaped and disappeared to pursue further adventures. What we do know is that Anne Bonny vanishes from the official records, leaving us to wonder if she ever thought of her comrade Mary in the years that followed.

Over time, the legend of Anne and Mary took on a life of its own. They've been depicted in books and artwork as a deadly, inseparable pair – two women blazing guns and bucking convention on the high seas. Were they lovers? We can't say for sure, but the very possibility has captured imaginations for centuries. After all, it's a tale almost too perfect: love and friendship kindled in the unlikeliest of settings, amid swashbuckling raids and tropical sunsets. Even if their relationship was purely one of deep friendship and loyalty, it was exceptional for its trust and equality. In an age when women were supposed to stay home and darn socks, these two dared to live wild and free, and possibly to love each other without a man in the equation. History meets Hollywood fantasy, indeed – their story practically begs for a big-screen adaptation with a sly romantic subplot.

Marriage lesson? A true partner in crime (literally, in their case) will stand with you through the fiercest storms. The saga of Anne and Mary shows that the strongest relationships are built on trust, shared adventure, and revealing your true self. Mary's bond with Anne truly solidified when she confided her identity – proving that honesty and vulnerability can spark a powerful connection. Their partnership thrived in conditions as rough as the ocean waves, so the everyday challenges of modern domestic life feel tame by comparison. If your love can survive sword fights, shipwrecks, and secrets, it can probably survive a frank talk about who forgot to take out the trash.

Frederick's Not-So-Great Secret – King Frederick the Great of Prussia favored male company and poetic bromances over royal duty – Enlightenment gossip swirled.

History remembers King Frederick II of Prussia as "Frederick the Great" – brilliant in war and philosophy, a ruler who put Prussia on the map. But behind the shine of his victories and reforms lay a not-so-great secret (or an open secret, if you eavesdropped on 18th-century gossip): Frederick much preferred the company of men, and his marriage was a sham he all but abandoned. He married a princess named Elisabeth Christine purely out of political duty and promptly kept her tucked away in a far-off palace like unwanted furniture. They had no children and almost never saw each other. By all accounts, he treated his wife with frosty indifference. The king was far more interested in his all-male circle of friends – his "philosopher fraternity," if you will – and in the camaraderie of handsome officers and cultured gentlemen who frequented his court.

The roots of Frederick's personal inclinations and his need for secrecy go back to his youth. As a crown prince, he was a sensitive soul who loved French art, music, and poetry – to the horror of his domineering father, King Frederick William, a man who valued soldiers and beer halls over sonatas and sonnets. Young Frederick formed an intense friendship with a dashing military page, Hans von Katte, and the two even attempted to flee Prussia together (whether they were running from Dad's tyranny or just planning a bro road-trip is up for debate). They were caught, and in a vicious display of "tough love," Frederick's father had Katte executed before the prince's eyes. Talk about trauma – it's like a tragic opera scene, except it really happened. After that, Frederick learned the hard way to keep his deepest feelings under lock and key.

Once he became king, Frederick crafted a life where he could almost be himself – as long as one read between the lines. He surrounded himself with male companions at his favorite residence, Sanssouci (his private palace whose name tellingly means "No Worries"). No ladies were allowed in this inner sanctum of music, conversation, and good wine. His neglected queen lived out her days quietly in another city, while Frederick filled his court with brilliant minds and attractive young officers. He struck up intimate friendships with his aides and confidants, penning them poems and affectionate letters. One Italian intellectual in his circle was nicknamed "the king's nightingale," and a particularly good-looking regiment adjutant might find himself rapidly promoted – perks of catching the king's eye. Enlightenment luminaries like Voltaire visited and observed the vibe; Voltaire later hinted (not so subtly) that Frederick's gatherings were more "gentlemen's club" than royal court in the traditional sense. The French philosopher Diderot outright joked that Frederick "never cared for women, not even his own wife." In diplomatic speak, that's calling him out as queer as a three-mark coin.

Of course, Frederick never officially "came out" – that concept didn't exist in the 18th century, and even a king had to maintain decorum. Publicly, he was the unmarried (in all but name) ruler married to his country. His image was that of a stoic, dedicated monarch who simply had no time for earthly passions (or so the court PR would have you believe). But people whispered in drawing rooms across Europe about the notoriously artsy, wife-avoiding King of Prussia and his "favorite" gentlemen. Frederick didn't much care what the whisperers said, as long as they didn't interfere. He had a country to modernize and wars to win; he could indulge his private life as he pleased behind palace doors. And indulge he did, albeit with the constant specter of scandal if anyone too important took offense.

Marriage lesson? Frederick's life is a study in what happens when societal pressure pushes someone into a marriage that's fundamentally at odds with their heart. He did his duty and married a woman, but neither of them got a real partner out of the deal – she got a lifetime of loneliness, and he spent his life pretending his heart was made of stone. The takeaway for us is simple: a marriage without genuine love or honesty is an empty shell. It's better to risk truth – to live authentically – than to trap yourself and others in a lie. We're fortunate to live in a time (at least in much of the world) where you don't have to be a Frederick, forced to hide your love and hurt others in the process. The old king with his secret poems and a wife he kept at arm's length reminds us that being true to who you are is not just a personal choice, but a moral one. Don't closet your heart – life's too short, even for a king, to pretend to be someone you're not.

Enlightened or Intolerant? – The 18th century launched modern anti-sodomy campaigns even as the aristocracy indulged same-sex love behind closed doors – a time of double standards and hidden queer culture.

So, was the Enlightenment truly enlightened about love and sexuality? The short answer: not by our standards. In fact, the 18th century saw some of the first organized moral crackdowns on queer communities, even as many high-born individuals kept right on with their same-sex romances in secret. On one hand, philosophers were championing the "rights of man" and the power of reason; on the other hand, "sodomites" (the era's nasty word for gay men) were being actively hunted down as if liberty and equality had some fine print attached.

In England especially, the climate grew harsher for gay men. Societies for the Reformation of Manners – basically morality police – sponsored raids to root out the underground gay subculture. They infiltrated molly houses and set up sting operations in parks or taverns. There was a spike in sodomy trials during the 1700s, fueled by these efforts. Punishments were severe. Some men were hanged after being convicted of "buggery" (as the law called it), and many more were sentenced to the pillory – a wooden contraption where the unlucky fellow was locked in and exposed to the public's wrath. Mobs would gather to jeer and throw rotten food, mud, even rocks. Men died in pillories, beaten or stoned by thugs who thought they were doing God's work. The message was clear: Enlightenment ideals of liberty did not extend to men who loved men, at least not at street level. It was a dangerous time to be anything other than strictly straight – especially if you lacked wealth or rank to shield you.

Meanwhile, the upper crust played by a different set of rules (as upper crusts usually do). A wealthy noble or a royal could often get away with behavior that would send a commoner to the gallows. They just had to keep it discreet and maintain a façade of respectability. We've seen examples: a king like Frederick could enjoy his all-male circle as long as he kept the official story intact. In British high society, there were certainly lords and ladies who had same-sex lovers or "romantic friends." The tacit agreement was to keep it behind closed doors and not scandalize polite society. If anything did leak out, families and connections rushed to hush it up. It was rank hypocrisy, of course – one law (or no law) for the rich, a very different law for everyone else.

Not everything was bleak, though. The seeds of progress were slowly being planted. Across the Channel in France, the revolutionary fervor brought a surprising reform: in 1791, Revolutionary France quietly decriminalized homosexual acts. It didn't exactly trigger a wave of rainbow flags (social attitudes take longer to change), but legally, France stepped into modernity while others lagged behind. And a few lone thinkers even mused that persecuting private love was cruel and irrational – a radical idea that foreshadowed changes still a century away. The bottom line is that the 18th century was a mixed bag: enlightened in science and politics, often intolerant in matters of sexuality. It created a thriving hidden queer culture – from the molly house gatherings in London to coded letters and poems exchanged between aristocratic lovers – precisely because official society pushed LGBTQ folks into the shadows.

Enlightened or intolerant? The era was both. It was enlightened enough to dream up universal rights, and intolerant enough to deny some people those rights in practice. The takeaway? A society isn't truly enlightened until it grants everyone the freedom to love. The 18th century's hidden romances prove that love endures even in intolerant times – a hopeful reminder that understanding can eventually triumph over ignorance.

Chapter 8

Victorian Secrets – The Love That Dared Not Speak Its Name

Ah, Victorian times – an era of stiff collars, stiffer moral codes, and *very* secret passions. Publicly, it was all "keep calm and carry a parasol," but behind those lace curtains and tailored suits lurked enough romantic intrigue to power a modern soap opera. The phrase "the love that dared not speak its name" really says it all: love was very much alive – it just had to whisper. In this chapter, we spill the tea (with two sugars and a dash of satire) on five fascinating stories of same-sex relationships in the Victorian age. From Oscar Wilde's courtroom fireworks to crafty ladies posing as "roommates," consider this a guided tour of the Victorian closet – with frequent detours for humor, pop culture parallels, and a few timeless marriage lessons sprinkled in. Ready to lift the veil on those Victorian secrets? Let's strut into the drawing room and begin, shall we?

Oscar & Bosie on Trial

Picture a Victorian celebrity scandal so juicy it would dominate Twitter – if Twitter had existed in 1895. At its center is Oscar Wilde: playwright, wit, *fashion icon* avant la lettre, and a man with a penchant for flamboyant velvets and even more flamboyant love. Oscar was the kind of literary superstar who could stroll into London's fanciest restaurant in a fur coat and command attention just by quoting one of his own epigrams (and he had *plenty* of them). Enter Lord Alfred Douglas, aka "Bosie," a young poet with golden curls, a rebellious streak, and a father who could give any reality TV stage-parent a run for his money. Oscar, in his forties, fell head-over-heels (perhaps head-over-spats?) for Bosie, who was half his age and twice his drama. They became the talk of the town – an open secret whispered in high society that this dapper duo were *more* than just pals who discussed French poetry over champagne.

Now, Victorian high society was all outward propriety and inward prurience. So while many *knew* about Oscar and Bosie, it was the kind of gossip exchanged behind fluttering fans at parties: "Oh, Lady So-and-So, did you hear about Mr. Wilde and that handsome young Lord? Scandalous!" The "love that dare not speak its name" – that poetic code for same-sex love – was on everyone's lips, even if only uttered in hushed tones. Ironically, Oscar himself ended up speaking its name loud and proud – in a court of law, of all places. How did we get there? Well, Bosie's father, the Marquess of Queensberry, was *not* about to send Oscar a "World's Best Son-in-Law" mug for Christmas. This was a man famous for creating the Queensberry rules of boxing, and he certainly approached his son's relationship like a boxer in the ring. Queensberry publicly accused Oscar of being a sodomite (spelling was not his strong suit; his infamous calling card read "posing somdomite"). Essentially, Dad went full troll mode, Victorian edition – leaving nasty notes and making scenes. Oscar, prideful and egged on by the hot-headed Bosie, decided to sue the Marquess for libel. Marriage Lesson: If your lover's parent is *that* determined to break you up, maybe eloping quietly is wiser than hauling the family drama into court. It's like choosing between a tense Thanksgiving dinner or a full-blown episode of Law & Order: Special Victorians Unit – Oscar unfortunately chose the latter.

The libel trial swiftly boomeranged on Oscar. To defend himself, Queensberry's side gathered evidence of Oscar's relationships with men – love letters, witty notes that suddenly looked less witty in the prosecutor's hands, and testimony from those pulled into Oscar and Bosie's wild orbit. Victorian London sat spellbound as intimate details of Oscar's secret life were paraded in open court. The scandal sheets had a field day; it was the 19th-century equivalent of a celebrity sex tape leak combined with a Broadway opening. One minute Wilde was the toast of the West End with *The Importance of Being Earnest*, and the next he was the defendant in "The Trial of the Century." Imagine if a beloved Oscar-winning screenwriter today was dragged into court over his Grindr messages – that's the level of gawking fascination. People packed the courtroom's public gallery as if it were opening night of a hit play. And in a way, it was: Oscar, ever the performer, delivered lines that would go down in history.

During his cross-examination, he was asked about that now-famous phrase, "the love that dare not speak its name." It came from a poem by Bosie himself, but now it was being used as a euphemism for their relationship. In a breathtaking moment, Oscar gave an impassioned speech defending the love of an older man for a younger as something noble and pure, comparing it to mentorships and artistic bonds – citing historical figures and speaking with the kind of eloquence that had people in the gallery actually applauding. Yes, Victorian jurors heard what amounted to a heartfelt TED Talk on gay love, courtesy of Mr. Wilde. Talk about courage! He basically said,

"You call it unnatural, I call it beautiful." If there'd been mic-drop technology in 1895, Oscar would have used it right there.

Alas, witty monologues don't sway juries when Victorian morals are at stake. Oscar's libel case collapsed (turns out suing someone for calling you gay is a bad plan if you, well, *are* and they can prove it). The tables turned, and soon Oscar was arrested and put on trial for "gross indecency" – essentially for being intimately involved with men. The spectacle only grew: two trials (the first jury hung, the second convicted him) full of salacious evidence and quips. At one point, asked about an incriminating detail, Oscar replied with his trademark sass, "I never travel without my diary. One should always have something sensational to read on the train." The man couldn't turn *off* the wit, even with his freedom on the line. It was like watching a tragicomic play where the lead actor can't help delivering zingers while the set collapses around him.

In the end, the verdict was *guilty*. Oscar Wilde was sentenced to two years of hard labor in prison – a punishment as brutal as it sounds. Bosie, the lover who had initially goaded Oscar into that ill-fated lawsuit, fled to the Continent, leaving Oscar to bear the brunt alone. It was a heartbreaking finale worthy of one of his own melodramas. Society, which had laughed at Oscar's plays, now laughed at *him* or turned away in horror. This love story didn't get a happy ending – more like a prison door slam and a sad fade-out. A once sparkling wit was broken by two years in Reading Gaol (where he wrote the haunting *Ballad of Reading Gaol* and a soul-baring letter, *De Profundis*).

Yet, in the ashes of that tragedy, Oscar Wilde became a martyr and icon for queer history – proof of how destructive societal hypocrisy can be. The "love that dared not speak its name" had been dragged through the mud, but it had also been spoken of with unforgettable eloquence. Marriage Lesson: Sometimes love means taking a stand, but timing is everything – pick your battles wisely. And perhaps the domestic takeaway: if your partner's parent is as toxic as Bosie's dad, running off to Naples is a safer bet than inviting the drama in. Love makes us do wild things; just try not to let one of them be getting yourself jailed at the height of your career. Oscar & Bosie's tale is a cautionary one: passion is grand, but in a society that isn't ready, it can exact a hefty price.

Still, despite the sad coda, Wilde's spirit lives on in every quip about romance under repression. His story kicks off our Victorian secrets tour with a flourish – a reminder that even when love was forced into the shadows, some brave soul might just seize a spotlight and declare it for all to hear. Now, speaking of keeping love in the shadows, let's look at how Victorian women managed to hide lifelong loves in plain sight, no court trials required.

Boston Marriages

While Oscar and Bosie's romance exploded under public scrutiny, many Victorians found quieter ways to let love live – especially women who discovered the perfect cover in society's blind spots. Cue the phenomenon of the Boston Marriage: no, it's not a legally recognized union officiated by the mayor of Boston, and it's definitely not a Red Sox fan club initiation. This was the 19th-century term for two women setting up house together, independent of any man's financial support, and often (though the neighbors might not have realized it) independent of men *period*. Think of it as the Victorian version of lifelong "besties" who secretly share more than recipes and needlepoint. They might have been coded as "companions" or "dear friends," but we can read between the lines – or rather, between the lace curtains.

Why "Boston" marriage? The term caught on in New England circles (Henry James's 1886 novel The Bostonians famously depicted a passionate friendship between two women, inspiring the nickname). But the arrangement was hardly confined to Boston; it was happening across the U.S. and Britain too. Society was oddly accepting of women living together – possibly because it was assumed women were sexless angels who just needed someone to share the rent and pour the tea. (Victorian men, bless their hearts, often couldn't fathom that two women could be in love *with each other* – that idea simply didn't occur to many of them, including, rumor has it, Queen Victoria herself. More on Her Majesty's selective imagination later.) Thus, two unmarried ladies setting up a joint household raised few eyebrows. In a time when an unmarried woman past 30 was pitied as an "old maid," having a female friend to avoid eternal spinsterhood was seen as sensible. "Oh, those two? They're just spinsters keeping each other company – how charitable!" winked polite society. Little did they know, behind closed doors, some of these lady couples were as devoted and *domestically entangled* as any married pair in town.

Let's dish on a couple of real examples. Take Sarah Orne Jewett, a successful novelist in Massachusetts, and her partner Annie Fields, an accomplished editor's widow. These two women shared a home and a life, and even celebrated anniversaries of the day they "gave themselves to each other." That's right – they basically had a private wedding without the church or state, but with heartfelt vows and poetry. Jewett once wrote to Fields on their one-year anniversary, and it wasn't "Happy roommate-versary, pal!" It was more like (to paraphrase), *"Do you remember, darling, a year ago when we promised ourselves to one another?"* Darling! Promises! If that's not marriage material, Victorian society, then what is? They took care of each other through illnesses, traveled together – a true partnership. It's as if they read the Victorian marriage handbook and said, "we can do all that, minus the husband bit." And they did splendidly.

They were hardly alone. Across the pond in England, you had arrangements like the one between Eleanor Butler and Sarah Ponsonby – Irish aristocrats a century earlier who ran away to Wales to live together (earning the nickname "The Ladies of Llangollen"). By the Victorian era, their legend had inspired many, and such romantic friendships continued to blossom. Another power couple was Alice Baldwin and Katharine Loring – the latter was the devoted partner of Alice's brother Henry James's own sister, Alice James (keeping track of the Alices and Alices and Henrys is a task, but the point is, even the James family had a Boston marriage in their midst!). The pattern was clear: educated, strong-minded women found fulfillment in each other's company, building lives that looked, walked, and quacked like a marriage – just without the legal recognition or the pesky male dominance. Marriage Lesson: A successful marriage (or marriage-like arrangement) often boils down to partnership and understanding. These women proved you don't necessarily need a husband to have a "wifey" life – you just need the right person who'll split the housekeeping and share your dreams. And maybe coordinate petticoats with you for the next social.

In fact, some of these Victorian gal-gal unions were downright progressive on the equality front. Consider this: while many straight Victorian wives were legally subservient to husbands (their property, earnings, even bodies weren't fully their own), two women living together could craft whatever rules suited them. They both could be breadwinners if they had careers or inheritance. They made joint decisions about home decor (no man cave vs. she-shed fights here – maybe just a spirited debate on where to place the settee). They offered each other intellectual companionship. If one loved writing and the other gardening, they supported each other's passions without the era's usual gender roles getting in the way. Financial independence was key – those who could afford a Boston marriage were often educated or had inheritance. Picture two Victorian ladies in starched high-collar dresses high-fiving (metaphorically) over the fact that they answer to no man. It's like The Golden Girls, Victorian edition – if Dorothy and Blanche secretly exchanged vows and had to pretend to be "just roommates" when Sophia walked in.

Now, were all Boston marriages romantic/physical? Hard to know from the outside – Victorian decorum meant people didn't exactly publish tell-all memoirs of their love lives (Anne Lister aside, but we'll get to her in a moment!). Some probably were essentially platonic companions, others were clearly passionate. The beauty of it – and the comedy, really – is how oblivious or in denial the outside world could be. If two men tried to live together, eyebrows would skyrocket and suspicions of sodomy would abound. But two women? "Oh, how lovely, neither could find a husband, so they're basically kindly roommates in a long slumber party." Talk about hiding in plain sight! It's the ultimate loophole: society didn't see women as sexual beings with agency, thus these couples effectively said "Fine, underestimate us – we'll be over here living our best lives together." Marriage Lesson: Sometimes the secret to a lasting relationship is teamwork and a united front – even if that front is pretending "Oh no, we're definitely not a couple, heavens no!" to the nosy neighbors. In modern terms, it's like those celebrity same-sex couples who before coming out would say, "This is my very dear friend and longtime roommate" at red carpet events. Wink, wink. Victorian women basically invented the art of the euphemistic plus-one.

Of course, not everyone was entirely clueless. Close friends often knew or suspected the true nature of these bonds. Some supported them; others likely rolled their eyes or whispered gossip. But crucially, the authorities and the public at large had no legal or social scaffolding to persecute two women for cohabiting. There was no law on the books against lesbian relationships – in part because, legend has it, Queen Victoria refused to believe such a thing existed ("Women? Doing *what* with each other? Oh, don't be ridiculous!"). True or not, that tale underscores how invisible lesbian love was to the male gaze. And invisibility, in this case, provided safety. It's a delicious irony: in an age when a man loving a man could land him in jail (poor Oscar), a woman loving a woman could often carry on relatively unmolested, so long as they played the pronoun game right and didn't rock the boat.

So there you have it: Boston marriages – Victorian lesbian power couples who quietly defied the patriarchy while hosting very prim afternoon teas. They highlight a fundamental truth: love will cozy up wherever it can, even under society's nose. When life handed these ladies lemons (in the form of patriarchy and spinster-shaming), they made a delightful lemon chiffon together and shared it on their front porch, smiling sweetly as Mr. and Mrs. Grundy walked by none the wiser. Theirs was the love that *didn't* speak its name – because it didn't have to. It just *lived*, with a knowing smile and occasionally a discreet hand held in the parlor when no one was looking. Next, we turn from a love that stayed safely unspoken to a woman who wrote about her love in code, practically daring future generations to find out exactly what she was up to. Ready for a peek into a secret diary? Grab your decoder ring; we're going in.

Gentleman Jack's Diary

Every great era has its tell-all memoirist. For the Victorians, that title arguably belongs to Anne Lister of Shibden Hall – landowner, scholar, world traveler, seducer of ladies, and journal-keeper extraordinaire. If you haven't met Anne Lister yet, think of her as the lovechild of Jane Austen and James Bond, with a dash of Carrie Bradshaw's journal habit, all wrapped up in a bespoke gentleman's suit. They called her "Gentleman Jack" (behind her back, of course) because she eschewed the frilly bonnets and instead strutted around in black masculine-style attire, confident as any lord of the manor. She climbed mountains, managed her estate, debated politics – truly a woman ahead of her time – and crucially, she liked the ladies. Oh, and she wrote *everything* down in her diary, in excruciating (and at times, delightfully scandalous) detail. But since this is Victorian England, she naturally wrote the naughtiest bits in a secret code. Yes, Anne basically invented the encrypted personal blog long before the internet was a thing.

Let's set the scene: Early 19th century into the 1830s (a tad pre-Victorian overlapping into early Victorian, but close enough), Anne Lister is living her best life in Yorkshire. By "best life," we mean juggling a string of romances with women of her social circle and beyond. While her peers were fretting about finding a husband, Anne was out here wooing wives and widows. She had schoolgirl crushes that turned into adult liaisons. One of her early loves, Mariana, actually *married a man* (society's pressures and all), but kept up a secret on-off affair with Anne for years – complete with clandestine meetups and torrid correspondence. If there were gossip columns for the gentry's sapphic affairs, Anne would've been front-page news. Fortunately for her, no such columns existed (her neighbors had no clue Miss Lister's "close friendships" involved any bed-sharing), and she took pains to ensure her own written record was undecipherable to prying eyes.

Ah yes, the diary. Anne Lister's diary was not your run-of-the-mill "dear diary, today I knitted and had tea" affair. It spans *over four million words* (truly, the woman wrote like it was her full-time job – move over, Karl Marx and your measly long book; Anne filled dozens of volumes). About a sixth of it was written in her secret code, which she dubbed "crypt-hand." This code was a fiendish combo of algebraic symbols, ancient Greek letters, and other arcane squiggles. Basically, it was the Enigma machine of the 1800s, and only Anne (and later one trusted relative) had the key. In these coded passages, Anne spilled all the intimate details of her love life – and I do mean *intimate*. She recorded her flirtations, kisses, *and more*. Some entries would make a modern romance novelist blush. She developed her own sly vocabulary: for instance, she used the letter "X" to denote, ahem, achieving a certain climactic point in lovemaking. If she particularly enjoyed an encounter, she might put two or three X's. (Yes, Anne Lister essentially came up with an early rating system for bedroom fun – Rotten Tomatoes, meet Passionate Posies? – except it was just for her own recollection.) Reading her uncoded diary entries today, you find sentences like, "Had Jane stay over. Three crosses before breakfast – not bad for a Wednesday." Okay, I'm paraphrasing loosely, but truly she noted sexual escapades with a frankness that would shock her Victorian contemporaries. It's positively NSFW (Not Safe For Work) 1834 edition.

So, what did Anne do with all this romantic information (besides record it for posterity)? She acted on it! Our Gentleman Jack wasn't content with dalliances; she wanted a wife, as legitimately as she could have one, given the law wouldn't recognize it. Enter Ann Walker, a wealthy neighboring heiress who caught Anne Lister's discerning eye. Anne courted Ann (two Anns, no waiting) with the determination of Mr. Darcy pursuing Elizabeth Bennet – only imagine Darcy wearing a top hat and sturdy boots, and Elizabeth being an adorably shy woman also in petticoats. After much diary-angsting, seduction via love letters and strolls, a few lover's quarrels, and tender reconciliations, Anne Lister achieved what might be called the first lesbian wedding in British history (at least the first we know about in detail). In 1834, Anne Lister and Ann Walker took communion together at church in York, exchanged rings, and basically said, "We're married now, to heck with anyone who says otherwise." Of course, they didn't send out engraved invitations or have a legit certificate – this was a personal, symbolic ceremony. But to them, it was binding. They moved in together at Shibden Hall, effectively wife and wife. If that's not romantic, I don't know what is. It's like they hacked the system: "No legal gay marriage in 1834? Fine, we'll DIY our own!"

Their union was hidden in plain sight (Ann Walker was ostensibly just living with Anne as her "companion" – oh that word again). But make no mistake, behind closed doors they considered themselves married. Anne's diary entry on that day is triumphant. She wrote it in code of course – likely something like "Today united with my dearest A—, soul joined, ++++" (I can only imagine how many code symbols peppered that entry). And here's the kicker: the locals in Halifax, Yorkshire, *still whispered about Anne.* They didn't know about the private church moment, but they saw two unmarried women setting up house and they saw how masculine Anne was in manner. She was dubbed "Gentleman Jack" by some who thought her odd. Yet, no one dared openly confront her, partly because she was a formidable lady of property who just did not give a fig for their opinions. Truly, a queen (well, a king?) living among them.

Fast-forward: Anne Lister tragically died young (age 49, of a fever while traveling in what is now Georgia in Eastern Europe – she was adventuring to the end). Ann Walker was left heartbroken and, lacking Anne's protective presence, eventually had a breakdown and was forced into her family's care. It's a sad epilogue, but their time together was groundbreaking. And those diaries? They were hidden away at Shibden Hall. Decades later, a relative in the late 1800s stumbled on them and deciphered a bit. Upon realizing Aunt Anne had essentially written the *Victorian Lesbian Kama Sutra Meets Daily Planner,* the family promptly hid the diaries behind a panel, scandalized. They stayed buried (metaphorically) until the late 20th century when finally historians published them. Now Anne Lister is rightly celebrated; she's even got a fabulous TV series ("Gentleman Jack" – if you haven't seen it, picture a dashing woman striding around to a punk rock soundtrack, seducing ladies left and right, and breaking the fourth wall with witty asides. Yes, they made her life into something as bold as she was).

From Anne's story, we glean a universal truth: living authentically is priceless, but it may require some stealth in unfriendly times.

Marriage Lesson: Communication is vital in relationships – and boy, did Anne communicate…even if it was in a secret code only she could read. Perhaps one key to a lasting love is writing down your feelings, dreams, and yes, your grievances – just maybe keep it in a locked diary or encrypted file if you're in a hostile environment. Also, the importance of being on the same page: Anne found a partner willing to walk that unconventional path by her side. Their private "wedding" is a reminder that marriage is fundamentally about a commitment between two people, recognized in their hearts if not by law. On a lighter note, there's another lesson here: if you're going to chronicle your love life, consider adding some encryption – *especially* if your descendants might read it. (Imagine Grandpa's secret diary in code – sometimes ignorance for the family is bliss!)

Anne Lister's courageous life and pen give us a rare uncensored glimpse into Victorian same-sex love – in the bedroom, the drawing room, and at the altar (even if that altar moment was just between them and the Almighty). It's history with the juicy bits intact, and we are all the richer (and frankly, a bit entertained) for it. Now, not everyone had Anne's moxie to live openly with their "wife." Many couples had to deploy next-level subterfuge to stay together. In the next section, we'll explore some of the creative – at times downright theatrical – ways Victorian same-sex lovers masked their relationships. Get your disguises ready; it's time for a costume change.

Love in Disguise

Victorians were nothing if not inventive when it came to keeping up appearances. In an age obsessed with propriety, same-sex couples often became the ultimate undercover agents of love. Think of them as romantic secret agents in crinolines and top hats, devising cover stories more elaborate than a Mission: Impossible plot – all for the sake of being together. This section is all about those covert strategies: the "just good friends" façade, the "oh, we're sisters" ruse, and even the "opposite-sex marriage of convenience" gambit. If love is a battlefield, these couples dug trenches and donned camouflage (sometimes literally).

One popular disguise, particularly for women couples, was posing as relatives, usually sisters. It was a genius move: who would question two "sisters" living together, sharing a little cottage or flat? Victorian society found it perfectly normal for unmarried sisters to stay together for life, especially if no man was around to take care of them. So, many a lesbian pair simply introduced themselves as siblings or "cousins" and blended into the social wallpaper. No one was likely to demand they prove their DNA, after all. Imagine the sly smile behind closed doors when they'd say, "Oh, yes, my *sister* and I moved here last spring." Technically false, but emotionally? They were as close as family – closer, in fact. Strategic lying for love – approved! It's the kind of trick that would make a modern sitcom plot: two lovers fool the nosy landlord by acting like family. (Cue laugh track when the landlord leaves and they finally steal a kiss.)

Another layer of disguise was the marriage of convenience, especially among the upper crust. Here's the playbill: a gay man and a lesbian woman (or generally two people who weren't romantically interested in each other because each preferred their own gender) would marry each other to satisfy societal expectations, then quietly allow each other the freedom to pursue their actual loves. It's basically "I'll be your beard if you'll be mine." These were the original lavender marriages – except with actual lavender sachets in their wardrobes because, you know, Victorian moths. For instance, there were cases of known bachelors suspected of being "confirmed in bachelorhood" (wink) who did take wives late in life, perhaps as cover. Some wives likely knew the score and had their own arrangements on the side. And some people never married at all but kept a respectable solo front while having a same-sex partner clandestinely.

Consider the predicament of a Victorian gentleman who happens to love other gentlemen. If he's rich and titled, the pressure to marry and produce heirs is immense. So what to do? Perhaps marry a dear female friend who also wouldn't mind a platonic partnership – maybe she has a romantic friendship with a lady herself, or she simply prefers independence and a title without the bother of a husband's affections. They tie the knot, attend each other's family Christmases, and appear at society functions arm in arm. Then, when night falls or whenever excuses can be made, he toddles off to his gentlemen's club (not always for the cigars and brandy, mind you) and she retreats to her own private quarters or "visits a friend" for weeks at a time. It was the ultimate win-win sham… so long as everyone played their part convincingly. Granted, not every Victorian with a secret had the opportunity to arrange such a tidy deal – but it certainly happened.

Pop Culture Analogy: Think of it like two Hollywood actors in the 1950s, both gay, marrying to keep the studio happy and the tabloids off their backs. Rock Hudson had a brief marriage to keep up appearances – similarly, some Victorian LGBT folks found opposite-sex partners to act as decoys. It's like a Jane Austen novel ghost-written by Oscar Wilde: "It is a truth universally acknowledged that a single man in possession of a good fortune must be in want of a wife – even if he's really, really not."

And then we have the truly bold method of disguise: cross-dressing and living as the opposite gender to be with the one you love. This one took immense dedication – and often a lifetime of sacrifice. There are several accounts from the 19th century of individuals assigned female at birth who presented as men (sometimes termed "female husbands" in sensational newspapers) in order to marry women. Were they what we might today call transgender men? Some likely were living their authentic gender identity *and* happened to love women, so it was a two-birds-one-stone situation. Others might have been more motivated by the only viable path to live with their beloved openly. Either way, imagine the sheer chutzpah: cutting one's hair, donning trousers (risking arrest just for that, since women wearing men's attire was literally a crime in some places), adopting a new name like John or William, and keeping up that role every single day – at work, in the pub, at church – all so that you and your sweetheart can walk down the street arm in arm and no one bats an eye. It happened. One famous case in the U.S. (we'll momentarily step outside Britain, since Victorian-era same-sex love tricks knew no borders) was Lucy Ann Lobdell, who in the 1860s lived as "Joseph" Lobdell and took a wife. They lived for a time as husband and wife in a rural community, until their cover was blown and poor Lucy/Joseph was dragged through humiliating trials and even institutionalized. British newspapers, too, loved printing shock stories of "a FEMALE passing as a MAN to wed another WOMAN!" Readers gasped over their tea, but I suspect a few secretly thought, "Good for them, pulling that off as long as they did."

On the male side, disguising as female to be with a male lover was less common as a long-term arrangement (harder to sustain, perhaps, and men had more to lose if discovered). However, there was the notorious case of Fanny and Stella in London – two young men, Ernest Boulton and Frederick Park, who loved to dress in women's clothing and hit the town as their alter egos, Stella and Fanny. They were more about living their true fabulous selves than specifically about being a couple in disguise (in fact, one had a nobleman boyfriend). But their arrest in 1870 for cross-dressing was a sensation. Ultimately they were *not* convicted of any serious crime (since dressing up, while scandalous, wasn't illegal per se and the authorities couldn't prove they did more than look pretty). Their story isn't exactly a romantic triumph, but it highlights the culture of disguise that queerness sometimes took on in that era – performance and reality blending. For some, cross-dressing was a necessary performance to live a reality of love.

Then there were countless less dramatic cover-ups: gentleman A calling gentleman B his "valet" or "secretary" so they could travel together; lady C introducing lady D as her "companion" or live-in governess for her non-existent children. Some male couples simply maintained separate residences and alternated dinner parties, feigning just friendship (the amount of "bachelor friend" phrasing in obituaries was staggering – codewords everywhere). One British historian noted that when an obituary of a lifelong bachelor mentioned his "longtime close friend" who shared a house with him, it often implied a partnership. They truly had a language of hints and nods. (Much later, "confirmed bachelor" became a wink-wink euphemism for "gay man" – its roots in this era of disguise.)

The ingenuity knew no bounds. One could liken it to a farce on stage: *The Importance of Being Earnest* comes to mind again – mistaken identities, secret engagements, imaginary invalid friends as excuses to leave town (Bunburying, anyone?). Wilde's play was satire, but in real life many gay Victorians *were* "Bunburying" – inventing trips or people to cover up trysts. Perhaps you tell your family, "Oh, I must visit my dear friend in Brighton for a few weeks to improve my health by the sea." Sure thing – except the "friend" is your lover and the health improvement is really a heart aflutter.

All these disguises and tactics underscore how desperately they wanted to protect their love and also avoid scandal or prison. It was a high-stakes game of charades. Some pulled it off and lived peacefully into old age with their chosen partner, the truth only quietly acknowledged by a few. Others were exposed and faced ruin. The stress must have been enormous – it's hard to keep a lifelong secret, especially one as central as whom you love.

Marriage Lesson: In any time period, a key to a lasting union is often a united front – and boy, did these couples master that. They remind us that sometimes love requires strategy and a pinch of acting skill. Modern couples might fib about whether they watched the next episode of a show alone, but Victorian couples were out here fabricating entire identities. Talk about commitment!

131

One can't help but marvel at the creativity. It's a bit romantic, in a swashbuckling way, to imagine two lovers conspiring each night over candlelight: "Okay dear, tomorrow you'll be my cousin newly come to town. And I'll wear that dreadful bonnet Aunt Agatha gave me – that should discourage any suitors." It's also heartbreaking that they *had* to resort to these measures. The ideal of an honest, open relationship was denied to them by the era's mores. That said, many succeeded in carving out a piece of happiness under the radar. It's a testament to human ingenuity – love finds a way, if not through the front door, then perhaps clambering down the trellis in disguise.

As we applaud these covert love stories, we should also cast a glance at the larger forces that made such disguises necessary. Victorian morality didn't exist in a vacuum; it was a cultural export, too. The British Empire, in all its globe-spanning might, spread its laws and attitudes far and wide – including its fear and criminalization of same-sex love. Our final stop on this tour of Victorian love's underbelly looks at that global legacy. How could a society that secretly harbored vibrant queer lives also impose draconian anti-gay laws on the world? Grab your pith helmet and a rainbow flag, because the sun never sets on the Empire's Shadow.

Empire's Shadow

If the hypocrisy of Victorian society were an Olympic sport, Great Britain would have been a gold medalist. Nowhere is this more evident than in the tale of how Britain handled homosexuality at home versus in the vast expanse of its empire. It's a story of global contradiction forged in crinoline and colonialism – basically, "Do as Queen Victoria's government says, not as Her subjects rather *fabulously* do behind closed doors." Let's unpack this with our trademark wit (because if we don't laugh, we might cry at the injustice).

By the mid-19th century, the British Empire was at its peak – controlling territories on every continent except Antarctica (penguins mercifully escaped Victorian moral codes). And wherever Britain went, it shipped not only English tea and the English language, but also English laws – including laws criminalizing same-sex relations. Britain's own anti-sodomy law, which once prescribed the death penalty for men "buggering" each other, had been somewhat softened by the Victorian era (no more hangings for being gay after 1861, thank goodness – progress!). But they still had severe punishments: prison, hard labor, the pillory in earlier days, you name it. And crucially, in 1885 they doubled down with the Labouchere Amendment, outlawing any "gross indecency" between men, even in private – a vague catch-all that nailed Oscar Wilde and many less famous men.

With the imperial zeal of a door-to-door salesman from hell, Britain exported these laws across its colonies. India got Section 377 of the penal code in the 1860s, making homosexual acts a crime "against the order of nature." African colonies, Caribbean islands, Asian territories – all received lovely parting gifts of Victorian legal homophobia. It's the longest-lasting unwanted souvenir collection in history. In fact, a majority of countries that still outlaw homosexuality today can trace that straight back (or rather, *not straight*, pun intended) to British colonial statutes. It's like Britain handed out anti-gay laws as party favors on the way out. "Thanks for attending the Imperialism Gala, here's your coat and a law criminalizing love. Cheerio!"

Now, here's the twisted part. While Britannia was busy telling the world to get its moral act together, at *home* British society was doing a weird two-step. On the surface, yes, it was stridently anti-gay – thus all the subterfuge we've discussed. But underneath, there was a thriving, if secretive, queer subculture in Britain. London had its underground clubs and rendezvous. There were drag balls being thrown where men dressed as women and danced the night away, defying gender norms with an audacity that would make RuPaul beam. One such ball in Manchester in 1880 was so extravagant (picture a hall full of Victorian drag queens and likely some male-male couples waltzing) that when the police raided it, even a hard-nosed detective described the scene as "men in the most fantastic fashions, eight of them in the garb of women" with a kind of awe. They had a *nun as a bouncer* at the door (yes, a fellow in a nun's habit checking invitations – you can't make this up), black curtains on the windows, the whole clandestine shebang. If that isn't queer culture thriving in secret, what is? And let's not forget the infamous Cleveland Street scandal in 1889: a male brothel in London's West End servicing upper-class gents (including, rumor had it, Queen Victoria's own grandson, Prince Albert Victor). When authorities got wind of it, there was a hush-hush cover-up to avoid implicating the high and mighty. The brothel was quietly closed, a couple of low-level guys fled the country, and the aristocratic clients were politely never named. In other words, if you were powerful enough, even if caught literally with your pants down, the empire's elite would protect you to avoid embarrassment.

So while colonial officers were busy enforcing Victorian morality on "uncivilized" peoples abroad, those very same types back in London might attend a secret gentleman's party where Oscar Wilde regaled everyone with risqué jokes and young men flirted behind potted palms. Double standard much? It's like a parent who preaches strict curfews to their kids but sneaks out to party when the kids are asleep. Britain told its colonies, "We must uphold Christian values!" Meanwhile, half the British aristocracy was either quietly indulging in pleasures with their own sex or at least tolerating it within their class as long as it stayed discreet.

We also have to mention the ladies here: the empire's laws ignored lesbianism (again, thanks to Queen Victoria's "What? Women? Nah!" attitude), so technically women-loving-women weren't outlawed. But socially, colonial societies under British rule became far less tolerant of any deviation from straight marriage norms than perhaps they had been before. Many cultures prior to colonization had recognized transgender or homosexual practices in various forms (for example, India had a history of the Hijra community – neither man nor woman, often eunuchs, who had spiritual and social roles; some African societies had traditional roles for queer individuals too). The British came in and effectively said "Nope, none of that, it's barbaric or sinful." They imposed a rigid binary and a prudish outlook that often supplanted local customs. The legacy: even long after the empire crumbled, those attitudes stuck like a stubborn stain.

It's a rich irony that modern Britain is now generally seen as progressive on LGBTQ+ rights (heck, they had Elton John singing at royal events and legalized same-sex marriage in the 2010s), while many Commonwealth countries are still battling the Victorian-era ghosts in their penal codes. One could almost hear the Victorian ghosts chuckling, "We may have left, but our law lives on, mwahaha!" Thankfully, change is coming in many of those places – India, for one, finally scrapped that old Section 377 in 2018, basically saying "Take your Victorian nonsense back, we're in the 21st century." But the damage of that exported homophobia lingers in cultural attitudes.

As for the contradiction within Britain: eventually, the facade cracked. By late Victorian and into Edwardian times, more voices (like Edward Carpenter, an early gay rights advocate, and various members of the intellectual circles) started challenging the status quo. The Wilde trial itself, tragic as it was, planted seeds of doubt in some minds about whether such persecution was just. But legally, Britain wouldn't decriminalize homosexuality until 1967 – a long way off. The empire's shadow is long indeed.

Marriage Lesson (Global Edition): Enforcing a "one size fits all" morality on others while flouting it privately is a recipe for resentment and dysfunction – whether in a marriage or between nations. Healthy relationships, personal or international, require honesty and respect. The British Empire's approach was the opposite, and the fallout was toxic and long-lasting. Also, perhaps: what goes around comes around. The very colonies Britain lectured eventually turned around to say, "Actually, you gave us these anti-gay ideas, and now you have Pride parades while we struggle – care to help clean up this mess?" In a cosmic sense, Victorian Britain is like that prim and proper aunt who wrote the rulebook on etiquette, only to be caught years later with a secret diary of scandalous liaisons. Oh wait, that's literally Queen Victoria's family – there were hints even one of her daughters might have had a female partner, and various aristocrats certainly did. Hypocrisy, thy name is Empire!

On a human level, imagine being a queer person in colonial lands under Victorian rule: not only might you face traditional societal disapproval, now the law – the mighty British law – marked you as a criminal. Yet, you might hear rumors that in London there are clubs or bohemian circles where people like you find some acceptance. It's a cruel push-pull. The empire's official stance was puritanical, but its hidden heart, at least in certain metropolitan pockets, beat to a more rainbow rhythm (albeit in secret). That's an empire at war with itself in a way – exporting one image while living another.

So as we conclude our romp through Victorian secrets, what have we learned? The Victorian era, often caricatured as prudish and straight-laced, was in reality full of people who loved and lusted and lived outside the narrow norms – they just had to do it covertly. We've seen Oscar Wilde boldly declare his forbidden love and pay the price, women in Boston marriages creating their own happily-ever-afters under society's nose, Anne Lister writing a very juicy diary that would make Bridget Jones faint, countless couples donning disguises or concocting cover stories worthy of Oscar-winning screenplays, and an empire preaching morality while quietly indulging (and harshly punishing) in equal measure.

The "love that dared not speak its name" echoes through all these stories – sometimes whispered, sometimes shouted defiantly. And in each we find not just historical curiosity, but relatable themes: the lengths people will go for love, the resilience of those who build a life together against the odds, the absurdity of societies that try to legislate affection, and the timeless truth that authenticity, when it finally shines through, has the power to change the world (or at least make it a tad more honest).

In a humorous, roundabout way, Victorian same-sex couples taught us some stellar relationship skills: teamwork, creative communication, managing in-law drama, budgeting on two incomes, secret-keeping (okay, maybe not a recommended modern skill), and above all, unwavering loyalty. They navigated a world that refused to acknowledge them, yet they left behind evidence – letters, diaries, poems, shared graves, courageous trials – that proclaim, "We were here, and we loved." Debunking the myth that LGBT relationships are a newfangled modern trend, their histories shout the truth (even if coded or couched in euphemism) that love between men, between women, and beyond binary, has always been part of the human story – yes, even between those starched Victorian sheets.

So next time someone extols the "good old days" of Victorian virtues, feel free to crack a knowing smile. The good old days had plenty of *fabulous* secrets. Victorian lovers might not have been able to speak their love's name openly, but through wit, will, and a wink, they found ways to express it. And in their courage and cunning, there's not just a history lesson, but a bit of inspiration – and admittedly, some ripe material for comedy – for us all. After all, love, like murder in a Victorian penny dreadful, will out. And thank goodness it does, because what a boring world it would be without these untold (and now happily told) stories of rainbow-hued romance beneath the corsets and cravats. Marriage Lesson: Whether in 1895 or 2025, love thrives on authenticity, trust, and sometimes a shared secret or two. Just maybe be glad today you don't need to pretend your spouse is your "cousin" at dinner parties (unless you're into very weird roleplay). Cheers to the Victorian lovers – they dared, they hid, they fought, they persevered. And now their truth is spoken, with pride and with a laugh at the absurdity they endured. The love that once dared not speak its name has found its voice, and oh, what a story it can finally tell.

Chapter 9

Out of the Shadows – Twentieth-Century Twists and Turns

The twentieth century wasn't just airplanes, jazz, and moon landings – it was also a wild rollercoaster for same-sex couples stepping (and sometimes tiptoeing) out of the shadows. In this chapter, we'll ride through five incredible true stories that put to rest any myth that queer love is a modern invention. From a brazen Catholic wedding hoax in 1901 Spain to secret love letters on the WWII front, from 1950s undercover romances to the rebellious 1960s that set the stage for Stonewall, these tales come packed with humor, heart, and a few marriage lessons (with a wink, of course). Buckle up for some twists and turns – and keep your arms and legs inside the time machine at all times.

Elisa & Marcela's Big Catholic Wedding

Our first stop is Spain in 1901, where two schoolteachers pulled off a Catholic wedding so audacious it sounds like something out of a soap opera – or a Netflix special (spoiler: there is one). Meet Marcela Gracia Ibeas and Elisa Sánchez Loriga, a devoted couple living in a very conservative, very Catholic corner of the world. They were in love and determined to be together at a time when "till death do us part" was supposed to happen only between a man and a woman. So what did they do? They hatched a plan that would have made Shakespeare proud and the Pope do a double take.

Like all great heist plots, it started with a fake identity. Elisa disappeared from town under the pretense of a huge lovers' quarrel and a voyage abroad – only to "return" in disguise as a dashing male cousin named Mario. (Yes, we have a woman in 1901 pulling a Mrs. Doubtfire, minus the kids and plus a mustache.) Marcela played the part of the forlorn fiancée perfectly, telling everyone her dear cousin Mario was coming to marry her. Gossipers noted Mario oddly resembled Elisa in build, voice, and temperament – but hey, if the townsfolk wanted a wedding, a wedding they would get.

Elisa – now Mario – spent months perfecting the art of manliness: chopping her hair, lowering her voice, and swaggering about in a suit. With an altered baptism certificate and nerves of steel, "Mario" and Marcela approached a priest in A Coruña. On the 8th of June, 1901, in a quiet little church, they actually pulled it off. The priest pronounced them husband and wife, blissfully unaware that the groom was his former female parishioner in a well-tailored disguise. A wedding portrait was even taken: Marcela in a white gown and Elisa-as-Mario in a stiff collar and jacket. If Instagram had existed then, that sepia-toned selfie would've gone viral.

The honeymoon was short-lived. News of this "marriage without a groom" spread fast, and Spanish authorities were not amused. When the story hit the papers – imagine headlines like "Scandal in the Pews!" – our newlyweds became wanted outlaws. They fled Spain with only the clothes on their backs (and perhaps that trusty mustache), slipping into neighboring Portugal to avoid arrest. There they were briefly jailed, but public sympathy and the absurdity of the case led to their release. Wasting no time, Elisa and Marcela hopped a steamship to far-off Argentina, hoping to start life anew where no one knew their story.

After that, their trail grows faint. Rumors say Elisa even married a man in Buenos Aires to keep up appearances (talk about commitment to the bit), but eventually the pair faded into history's background. We'd like to imagine they lived out their days together quietly, clinking glasses to their extraordinary youth whenever anniversaries rolled around. One thing is certain: they managed a feat far ahead of its time. Spain wouldn't legalize same-sex marriage until 2005 – yet these two women got a church-sanctioned "I do" in 1901 with sheer bravery and love (and a few fibs).

Marriage lesson? If your love makes you brave enough to outwit an entire church and country, it's probably the real deal. (Just maybe don't try this at home – or at Mass – without a solid exit strategy.)

Paris, Stein, and Toklas

For our next tale, we trade Spanish villages for Parisian salons and switch genres from heist to bohemian rom-com. It's the 1920s in Paris – the Jazz Age – and hosting one of the most famous literary salons in history is an unconventional power couple: Gertrude Stein and Alice B. Toklas. They didn't have a marriage license (that wasn't an option), but their partnership had all the quirks and comforts of a long, happy marriage. In their home at 27 rue de Fleurus, they wined and dined the likes of Picasso, Hemingway, Fitzgerald – basically the Avengers of Modern Art – every week. And at the center of this glittering social circle were Gertrude, the larger-than-life avant-garde writer, and

Alice, her sharp-witted, doting partner who kept everything (and everyone) on schedule.

Stein was charismatic, loud, and unapologetically herself – a woman who talked as if every word were a pronouncement. Toklas, petite and reserved, was the quietly formidable force making sure Gertrude's brilliance didn't float off into chaos. If Gertrude was the eccentric diva holding court (picture a bohemian Oprah, perhaps), Alice was the stage manager and spouse combined, ensuring the candles were lit, the genius guests were fed, and her "wifey" Gertrude didn't say anything too outrageous (at least not before dessert). Friends quickly learned that while Stein might seem to dominate, Alice ran the show in her subtle way. There's a story that Hemingway overstayed his welcome one evening – until Alice pointedly said, "Gertrude, dear, it's bedtime," promptly ending the night. You can bet Papa Hemingway grabbed his hat in a hurry. In the Stein-Toklas household, Alice's word was law.

Their day-to-day life looked a lot like a marriage, too. They lived together for nearly four decades, settling into routines that would make any old married couple proud. Gertrude wrote late into the night; Alice rose early to type up Gertrude's pages and tend to domestic duties. They left each other affectionate notes around the house, often signed with pet names like "Lovey" or simply "Y.D." for "Your Darling." In letters, Gertrude referred to Alice as her "wife" long before society would catch up to that idea. They celebrated an anniversary every year – the day Alice first came to Gertrude's side – treating it with the seriousness of a wedding date. When Gertrude published *The Autobiography of Alice B. Toklas* in 1933 (essentially a memoir of their life together, cheekily written in Alice's voice), the world got a peek at their extraordinary bond. Suddenly, they were famous – and although newspapers coyly called Alice her "companion," it was clear these two were a package deal.

Through the tumult of two world wars and countless art movements, Gertrude and Alice remained devoted. When Stein fell ill with cancer in 1946, Alice was by her side day and night. Gertrude's last words were playful and philosophical (in true Stein fashion), but the heartbreak was real – Alice lost the love of her life. Yet even in death, they stayed side by side: Alice arranged to be buried next to Gertrude in Paris's Père Lachaise Cemetery. Gertrude's name is on the headstone in bold; Alice's name is engraved on the back, a quiet second billing she was content with, as always.

Marriage lesson? Gertrude and Alice proved that a marriage of minds and hearts doesn't need official papers to thrive. They balanced each other beautifully – one bright star and one steady compass. Every marriage has a bit of Gertrude and a bit of Alice: one partner with the big ideas, and one making sure the laundry gets done and the guests go home on time. The secret sauce is love and mutual respect (and maybe the occasional firm "bedtime, dear" to keep things on track).

Love Letters in a Time of War

Now we turn to World War II, where amid the gunfire and blackouts, two star-crossed British soldiers kept their love alive through pen and paper. This is the story of Gilbert Bradley and Gordon Bowsher, who exchanged hundreds of secret letters during the 1940s. Think "The Notebook" meets "Brokeback Mountain," but with censors and court-martial risk as the villains. At that time, being gay in the military was beyond forbidden – it was a criminal offense, punishable by prison, disgrace, even execution in extreme cases. Yet Gilbert and Gordon didn't let that stop them from pouring their hearts out to each other, one postage stamp at a time.

Every letter was a lifeline. "My own darling boy," one began, in handwriting that surely trembled with both love and fear. In another, one of them confessed, "There is nothing more I desire in life but to have you with me constantly..." These weren't just battlefield updates or stiff-upper-lip platitudes; they were full-on love letters, the kind that could make even a stoic colonel blush. The catch was, they had to keep everything under wraps. Gordon signed his letters simply "G" to avoid detection. Gilbert would hide these precious pages like contraband, knowing a routine barracks inspection could destroy their lives. It's hard to overstate the courage behind each "I love you" they dared to write.

Perhaps the most hopeful line came in one of Gordon's letters: *"Wouldn't it be wonderful if all our letters could be published in the future in a more enlightened time? Then all the world could see how in love we are."* In 1940, that wish must have seemed as fantastical as a fairy tale. But flash forward seven decades: after Gilbert's death, those very letters were discovered in an old trunk and made public. The world finally saw their love, and instead of scandal, readers found it beautiful and poignant. The "more enlightened time" Gordon dreamed of had finally arrived.

Gilbert and Gordon's wartime romance didn't get a traditional happy ending in the 1940s – the pressures of society were too great, and they went their separate ways after the war. Yet, through those letters, their love endures as a time capsule of hope. Reading them today, we're reminded that even when the world tries to outlaw love,

love quietly persists in the shadows, waiting for the day it can shine openly.

Marriage lesson ? Communication, communication, communication ! These two maintained a profound connection using only pen and paper (and unflinching honesty) under circumstances that would test any couple. If they could keep the flame alive from afar in such darkness, surely we can manage to text back our partners promptly. And their dream of a brighter future for love shows the power of hope – sometimes the lovers of today are writing the script for a more accepting tomorrow.

Lavender Scare and Bold Care

The post-war 1950s in America brought prosperity for some – and paranoia for others. Alongside the Red Scare (fear of communists) came the Lavender Scare – an officially sanctioned witch hunt for homosexuals, especially in government service. In 1953 the President even banned LGBTQ folks from federal jobs, deeming them "security risks" (as if the Kremlin's top spies were lurking in gay bars instead of, you know, stealing state secrets). Police raided queer-friendly bars, newspapers outed suspects with shameless glee, and "Are you now or have you ever been gay?" was the unspoken question ruining lives. It was a cruel irony: after fighting fascism abroad, countless queer Americans came home only to be treated as enemies of the state for the crime of loving someone.

Yet even under this pressure, same-sex couples refused to disappear – they just got creative. This era saw the rise of the strategic "beard" and the revival of the old "Boston Marriage" in modern form. Gay men might marry straight women (sometimes lesbian friends in on the plan) so both could enjoy societal respectability by day and their real loves by night. Others avoided matrimony but kept a "girlfriend" or "boyfriend" as cover when needed. Likewise, two women in a "Boston Marriage 2.0" would set up house as "roommates" – often introducing one partner as a "cousin" or "dear friend from college" to dodge prying eyes. Neighbors might chuckle about the confirmed bachelors down the street or the spinsters who never married, but as long as appearances were kept up (separate bedrooms staged for show, twin beds just in case Mom visited), society's don't-ask-don't-tell vibe provided a thin shield.

Behind closed doors, love found a way. Same-sex couples built underground support networks and code words. They threw private parties where, for a few golden hours, men danced with men and women romanced women without fear – the windows curtained, the record player turned up to drown out whispers. In living rooms across the country, activist seeds were being planted. Groups like the Mattachine Society and the Daughters of Bilitis started as secret gatherings of a few brave souls. They discussed how to survive, maybe even how to insist on their dignity. Members often arrived in pairs – quiet couples determined to help create a world where they could simply be together without a charade.

Of course, hypocrisy abounded: even J. Edgar Hoover, the FBI director who fueled much of the Lavender Scare, was widely believed to be in a cozy lifelong relationship with his male deputy. (Apparently it was fine to be gay as long as you hunted other gay people – go figure.) But many same-sex love stories of the 1950s never made the headlines; they were lived in everyday acts of devotion. A stolen kiss in a darkened doorway, a hand squeeze under the dinner table when the relatives made a crass joke – couples cherished what moments they could. And when one partner got in trouble, the other would spring into action, even if that meant rounding up bail money after a bar raid or concocting an alibi on the fly.

Marriage lesson? Sometimes it's truly "us against the world." The mid-century couples taught us the value of solidarity and ingenuity in a relationship. They learned to communicate in code, to shield each other, and to build a life in the margins with love and humor intact. Modern couples might not need secret twin beds and code names (phew!), but the trust and teamwork those duos mastered are inspirational. When life gets tough, a couple that sticks together and has each other's back can weather just about any storm.

The Dam Begins to Break

By the mid-1960s, the tide was finally turning. The Civil Rights movement and women's liberation were in full swing, and the LGBTQ community felt a new electricity in the air. After so many years in hiding, cracks began to appear in the dam of silence. Couples ever-so-cautiously started stepping into the light. Some dared to hold informal wedding ceremonies with close friends as witnesses – private celebrations of love with no legal standing, but plenty of champagne and courage. A few daring souls even walked hand-in-hand in public in progressive enclaves, turning heads and quietly saying, "We're here, and we're not ashamed." It was risky, yes, but these small acts were the seedlings of a revolution.

Activism was also heating up. In 1965, a handful of brave activists picketed outside Independence Hall in Philadelphia carrying signs that politely demanded equality for "Homosexual Americans."

Among them were same-sex couples who dressed in their Sunday best and stood side by side, determined to show the world they were ordinary folks who loved each other – not monsters, not deviants, just people. Around the same time, a fired government astronomer-turned-activist named Frank Kameny coined the slogan "Gay is Good." It was a simple phrase with the radical idea that gay people should be proud of who they are. That motto caught on, fueling picket lines and discussions in coffee houses. For the first time, LGBTQ couples began to see a future where they might love openly without fear.

The momentum built to a climax in June 1969 at a little Greenwich Village bar called the Stonewall Inn. When police raided this popular gay hangout one hot night – a routine harassment that folks had endured for years – the patrons unexpectedly fought back. The uprising that followed, led by drag queens, gay street kids, lesbians, and allies, lasted for several nights and signaled that the community was done living in the shadows. Amid the clash with police, you can bet there were couples in that crowd – lovers who had tasted freedom inside the bar now refusing to let it go. One famous story has a woman in masculine attire, fed up with being manhandled, shouting to onlookers, "Why don't you guys do something?" – a call that ignited the crowd. Do something they did. The Stonewall Riots became the thundercrack that broke the dam wide open.

In the wake of Stonewall, LGBTQ life would never be the same. Within a year, couples who once only whispered about commitment were marching openly in the streets of New York, Los Angeles, and beyond in the first Gay Pride parades. They carried banners, held hands, even kissed in front of City Hall – acts that seemed unthinkable a decade prior. The love stories that had long been forced underground were now dancing on top of the dam's debris, jubilant and unafraid. The stage was set for a new chapter of liberation.

Marriage lesson? Love is resilient, and when enough people share that love openly, it can change the course of history. The 1960s showed that personal courage in relationships – be it daring to call your partner "dear" in public or standing together at a protest – it can ripple outward and become social change. Sometimes the strongest foundation for progress is the simple bond between two people who refuse to let go of each other, come what may. And as the saying goes, "love conquers all" – in this case, love helped conquer fear, paving the way for the world we know today.

Chapter 10

Pride and (No) Prejudice – Modern Love, Myths Debunked, and History's Echo

Stonewall to Rainbow Weddings

Picture it: New York City, June 1969. In a little bar called the Stonewall Inn, the DJ is spinning Motown, the fashion is fabulous (think Judy Garland mourners mixed with hippie chic), and *bam!* – in storm the police for yet another raid on the gay community. But this time, instead of cowing and handing over IDs, the patrons decide "not today, officer." A scuffle breaks out, a brick flies (legend says a heroic drag queen or two were involved), and what started as a routine harassment turns into a full-blown uprising. The Stonewall Riots lasted several nights – a glitter-fueled "we're mad as hell and not gonna take it anymore" moment that essentially shouted to the world that LGBTQ+ folks weren't going to stay in the shadows. It was as if the Avengers assembled, but in bell-bottoms and with a lot more mascara. That defiant stand echoed through history's corridors and is now commemorated each year as Pride – basically the anniversary party of the moment queer people fought back.

Fast forward to the first anniversary: June 1970, the streets of New York (and LA, and Chicago) see the first Pride marches. These weren't the technicolor parades we know today with corporate sponsors and drag queens on floats; they were more like protest walks with catchy slogans and homemade signs. Yet, even then, there was joy in the air – an *in-your-face* celebration of identity. Over the years, these marches evolved into the full-blown Pride parades of today: part political rally, part Mardi Gras, part family picnic (yes, kids and all). By now, Pride is so mainstream that you'll see your bank, your grocery store, and even your local police dept decking out in rainbow logos each June. (Corporate America loves a rainbow if it sells – who knew the revolution would be brought to you by breakfast cereal and insurance companies?) The irony isn't lost: what once was underground is now *the* annual block party. It's like the world went from "don't say gay" to handing out rainbow swag bags. Progress, indeed.

But Pride isn't just parades – it's paved the way to something once unthinkable: rainbow weddings on a grand scale. After decades of activism, legal battles, and probably a million repetitions of "love is love," countries around the globe began to legalize same-sex marriage. The Netherlands led the way in 2001, casually becoming the first country to say "Sure, let the two brides kiss!" (Leave it to the Dutch, with their famously chill attitudes, to be first. They gave us tulips, Van Gogh, and now gay marriage – truly trendsetters.) One by one, other nations followed: Canada said *"eh, why not"* in 2005, Spain shouted *"¡Sí, queremos!"* the same year, South Africa – yes, in the continent where it was once *illegal* – broke barriers in 2006. Even traditionally conservative places started coming around. Ireland – *Ireland!* – historically Catholic and not exactly known for wild social liberalism, shocked the world in 2015 by voting in a landslide to legalize same-sex marriage by popular vote. It was as if St. Patrick himself returned to say *"love who you want, lads and lasses"*. The United States took a while, but in 2015 the Supreme Court finally made marriage equality the law of the land nationwide, and the White House lit up in rainbow colors that night like it was throwing a Wizard of Oz-level Technicolor after-party. At this point, dozens of countries allow same-sex couples to wed, from Taiwan to Germany to Brazil. What started at Stonewall as a fight for basic dignity blossomed into full legal recognition – talk about a glow-up for the ages.

The best part? Those long-term couples who had loved each other through decades when their love had to dodge both disapproval and the law suddenly got to make it official. Picture those heartwarming scenes: two men in their 80s holding hands at a city hall, tearing up because after 50 years together, they're finally signing a marriage license. Or two adorable old ladies in Iowa – in their 90s no less – who met during World War II and had to keep their relationship a secret for *72 years*, finally able to say "I do" in front of a crowd of cheering friends and family. (True story: Vivian Boyack and Alice "Nonie" Dubes did just that, proving that patience is a virtue and love truly endures. They basically waited an entire lifetime for the law to catch up with them – talk about commitment! If you ever feel your partner is slow to propose, just think of Vivian and Alice.) These scenes played out all over: couples who once would have been *arrested* for dancing together in the 50s were now dancing at their weddings to "At Last" by Etta James. It's the kind of plot twist that history rarely delivers, and it was real.

With weddings come families, and indeed the rise of LGBTQ+ family life has been another joyful chapter. Once upon a time, the idea of two dads or two moms raising kids was fodder for outrageous "what-if" debates on talk shows. Now, it's increasingly just another normal Tuesday. Same-sex couples are raising children everywhere – through adoption, surrogacy, blending families – and doing it with the same mix of love, exhaustion, pride, and panic as any other parents. We see famous gay dads and moms on TV and in real life: Elton John and his husband David furnish their life with two little boys; Neil Patrick Harris and his husband post ridiculously cute Halloween family portraits with their twins; Wanda Sykes cracks jokes about the chaos of motherhood with her wife in comedy specials. Even a sitting U.S. Cabinet member, Pete Buttigieg, proudly took parental leave to care for his newborn twins with his husband – and the nation mostly said "Aww." (Sure, a few cynics grumbled, but they got drowned out by the collective cooing over baby pictures on Twitter.) The lesson here? The sky didn't fall when gay couples started having families. In fact, it got a bit more fabulous and a lot more *normal*. Kids in playgrounds today casually mention their two moms or two dads, and their friends might only be jealous that this means double the parental backup to plead for snacks. Modern family life now comes in all flavors of the rainbow, and that echoes through our culture: children's books feature same-sex parents; big companies offer partner benefits and parental leave to LGBTQ employees; even Disney eventually included openly gay characters in their movies (finally catching up to what kids see in their own neighborhoods). It's as if the world collectively realized that letting people love who they love and form families isn't the end of civilization – if anything, it's an expansion of it.

Marriage lesson: Love, patience, and persistence pay off. Sometimes you wait 72 years, but that kiss at the altar makes it all worthwhile. And if anyone crashes your wedding with negativity? Just channel the spirit of Stonewall and politely (or not so politely) show them the door.

Myth Busted – "It's a Modern Phase"

Every so often, you hear someone sigh and say, *"Ugh, this whole gay thing is just a modern trend. In my day, people weren't gay – or if they were, they kept it to themselves."* According to this myth, same-sex love is like man-buns or TikTok dances – a fad that showed up the day before yesterday and will vanish tomorrow. Well, fasten your historical seatbelt, because we're about to time-travel and prove that notion as wrong as thinking the Earth is flat (which, funnily enough, is another myth that keeps resurfacing – but that's another chapter).

Same-sex relationships have existed across millennia, cultures, and continents – basically, as long as humans have been humans (and honestly, even some animals pair up gay, but we'll stick to human history for now). If being queer is a "phase," it's the longest phase in the history of ever. We're talking a phase that spans from ancient pharaohs to modern pop stars. It's older than the pyramids – literally. In fact, archaeologists in Egypt discovered what might be one of the oldest recorded same-sex couples: two royal male officials from around 2400 BCE (yep, the *Bronze Age*). Their names were Niankhkhnum and Khnumhotep – try saying that three times fast – and they were buried together in a shared tomb, depicted in intimate poses usually reserved for married couples. On the wall, they're shown touching nose-to-nose in a loving embrace (the ancient Egyptian equivalent of a kiss emoji). Now, does that sound like a "modern phase"? These guys were likely cozying up to each other before the Great Pyramids even had a fresh coat of paint. If Twitter existed then, #LoveIsLove would be written in hieroglyphs.

Moving forward a bit, ancient Greece is practically famous for its same-sex relationships. We often joke about "Greek culture" and wink, but truth is, the Greeks didn't even have a concept of "gay" the way we do – it was just one of the many ways to love. Sure, they had social norms (like older mentors with younger protégés in something called pederasty – a practice we rightfully frown on today). But adult same-sex love was celebrated too. The poet Sappho, around 600 BCE, was basically the Adele of her day, writing passionate love poems... to other women. In fact, she lived on the island of Lesbos, which is why we have the term "lesbian" today. Sappho's poems survive only in fragments, but what we have is steamy enough to leave little doubt she was head over heels for the ladies. So next time someone claims lesbians were "invented" in the 20th century, remind them that a Greek woman was dropping lyrical love lines to her girlfriend when the Parthenon was still under construction.

And it wasn't just Greece. Ancient Rome was no slouch in the same-sex love department either. Many Roman men and women pursued same-sex flings or lifelong loves, often without much fuss. Several emperors had male lovers or favorites. They were too busy conquering and throwing lavish parties to bother with who was sleeping in whose villa. For example, Emperor Hadrian (we'll gossip more about him later) basically took a grand tour of the empire with his beloved boyfriend in tow, and most Romans shrugged or even admired the cute couple. Love was love, or at least a strong like – they didn't send out rainbow wedding invites, but it was common enough not to write home about. Romans cared more if you were polite, paid your debts, and wore your toga correctly in public – not so much about the gender of your beloved.

Hop over to Asia: in ancient China, same-sex love had poetic nicknames like "the passion of the cut sleeve" and "bitten peach." Those aren't code for trendy cocktails; they're references to stories of imperial male lovers. One famous tale involves an emperor in the Han Dynasty (around 1st century BCE) who was so smitten with his sleeping male companion that when he needed to get up, rather than disturb his lover, he cut off the sleeve of his own robe under which the young man was napping. People in court *awed* at this and "cut sleeve love" became shorthand for male-male romance. Another tale tells of a nobleman sharing a peach he had half-eaten with his male crush – and that "leftover peach" became a symbol of affection between men. These were well-known cultural stories, meaning nobody found them bizarre. If anything, they set a kind of romance standard in literature. Imagine a modern rom-com but with flowing robes and swords; that's Chinese love stories, and they included gay ones without batting an eye.

Over in Japan, by the medieval period, they had something called "shudō", a tradition where a young samurai would have an older samurai as a mentor and lover. These relationships were often deeply emotional and yes, sexual, and were even thought to enhance bravery. (Think about it: you and your lover going into battle side by side – that's some epic Bonnie-and-Clyde, or rather, Ben-and-Clyde energy right there.) Far from being shunned, this was part of the samurai code for some; they wrote about it in romantic tales and war epics alike. A samurai diary might read like: "Today, practiced sword-fighting, wrote a haiku, cuddled with my companion under the cherry blossoms. Life is good." Not a "modern phase" by any stretch – more like a longstanding tradition.

Let's not forget the numerous cultures of the Americas and Africa pre-colonialism. Many Native American tribes revered individuals who we'd now call LGBTQ+. The term "Two-Spirit" is used to describe people who embodied both masculine and feminine qualities, and often these folks could have relationships with same or other genders without stigma; in fact, they were frequently honored as healers or wise persons. Similarly, in parts of Africa before certain religions took hold, same-sex relationships and fluid gender roles existed in various forms – they were just part of the social fabric. In other words, the idea that "society" had never seen two women or two men in love until circa 1970-something is pure fiction. It's like claiming nobody ever ate avocados until avocado toast came along. Nope – it's been around; you just didn't notice it in the history books.

So why do some people today think it's "just a trend"? Probably because for a few centuries (looking at you, colonial era and Victorian prudery), these relationships were forced underground and written out of the official narratives. History got a bit one-sided (the straight side) in the retelling, making it seem like LGBTQ folks popped up suddenly like dandelions after a rain. In reality, they were always there like wildflowers in the field – just sometimes trampled or hidden. But make no mistake, same-sex love is ancient. It's as *OG* as it gets. If it were software, we'd be on Version 10.0 by now with regular updates.

Marriage lesson: Don't fall for the "phase" nonsense. Love that lasts thousands of years isn't a phase; it's a human feature. Trends come and go – platform shoes, pet rocks, the Ice Bucket Challenge – but love between consenting adults, regardless of gender? That's a classic. Timeless, like a little black dress or a well-tailored suit, and it's here to stay.

Myth Busted – "They Didn't Have Real Sex Back Then"

Alright, let's address the giggle-inducing myth that ancient or historical same-sex couples were just *platonic pals* who maybe cuddled at most, but certainly didn't do the deed. This idea basically paints people in history as prudish Barbie dolls with no genitalia when it came to same-sex encounters. Time to set the record straight (or rather, not straight): our ancestors were as frisky, curious, and *inventive* about physical love as we are – possibly more so, since they didn't have the internet for…er, inspiration.

First off, if you think same-sex love in history was all chaste hand-holding and longing glances, ancient literature would like a word. Take the Kama Sutra, that famous guide to love and pleasure compiled in India around the 3rd century CE. Many people think of it as just a straight manual (in both senses of the word) for spicing up the bedroom, but guess what – it has entire sections on homosexual acts. Yes, indeed. The Kama Sutra acknowledges and describes sexual techniques between men, and between women, with a matter-of-fact tone that suggests *"Yeah, people do this. Enjoy."* Lesbian women are referred to as "swarinis" in this text, and they're depicted as fully capable of satisfying each other. Men engaging in oral sex with other men are described as well, with no horror or scandal – just as another category of intimacy. So, over 1,500 years ago, a best-selling (so to speak) self-help sex book was basically saying, *"Here's how you do it, whatever your orientation."* They definitely weren't leaving those chapters blank. If ancient Indians recognized it and even gave pointers, you can bet "real sex" was happening back then.

Now, let's get visual – because ancient people left us some pretty R-rated art to prove the point. In the ruins of Pompeii, the Roman city frozen in time by a volcanic eruption, archaeologists found explicit frescoes and graffiti that would make a modern sailor blush. Among the gems: naughty poetry about guys hooking up with guys, and even drawings that are basically the first-century equivalent of bathroom stall caricatures of same-sex encounters (yes, human nature hasn't changed *that* much). And what about the Greeks? Well, they decorated some of their pottery with images of men getting very friendly with each other, shall we say. Wealthy Greeks sipping wine at a symposium (basically a booze-fueled philosophy party) might pass around cups that had erotic scenes – including male-male ones – painted on them. One famous artifact, the Warren Cup (now in the British Museum), features not one but two different male/male couples in rather acrobatic embraces. Clearly, the idea of what "sex" entails was not limited to hetero definitions. The artists captured the… er… full monty of possibilities. If those pots could talk, they'd wolf-whistle.

If museum trips aren't your thing, consider temple art. Across parts of India and Southeast Asia, there are temples built over a thousand years ago with highly detailed erotic carvings. The temples of Khajuraho in India, for instance, are famous for their sculpture panels of people intertwined in every which way. Among these candid stone snapshots are depictions of women with women and men with men enjoying intimate moments. Imagine a tourist squinting up at a 10th-century temple facade and going, "Are those… two guys?" Yes, yes they are. In one carving, a man is clearly in a sensual situation with another man in a group scene (we'll leave it at that), which tells us the sculptors of the day were not shy about the full spectrum of love. The existence of these images isn't because some modern prankster went around carving them in later – they're original. Apparently, "No hetero" was also part of the ancient karma sutra ethos carved in stone for all to see.

And let's address the ladies, because some skeptics think historical women who were close were just BFFs braiding each other's hair. Oh, they braided hair alright – and then some. Ancient Greek literature gives us the example of Sappho and her female lovers (those poems didn't survive because they were G-rated friendship sonnets, trust me). In Rome, there are accounts (though fewer) of women enjoying other women. The satirist Lucian in the 2nd century even wrote a saucy dialogue where a courtesan gleefully describes her affair with a woman from Lesbos, saying her lady lover was far better in bed than any man she'd known. Mic drop from antiquity! Even in medieval times, there are hints: nuns writing strangely passionate letters to each other, or that famous case of two women in the 18th century Ireland, the "Ladies of Llangollen," who eloped and lived together – people called them romantic friends, but you read their diaries and it's clear there was more than embroidery going on at bedtime.

Perhaps the myth comes from the prudish sensibilities of later eras that couldn't imagine our forebears being so *scandalous*. But really, people in the past had fewer sources of entertainment. No

Netflix, no TikTok – they had to make their own fun. And boy, did they ever. From emperor Nero who in the first century AD married a man in a public ceremony (he literally took a young man named Sporus, castrated him, dressed him up as a bride, and married him before the whole imperial court – Romans never did anything by halves) to the sailors and soldiers throughout history known for the phrase "any port in a storm" with a wink, there was plenty of real sex happening of all orientations. Were there periods of hush-hush and coded language? Sure. Oscar Wilde in the Victorian era had to call it "the love that dare not speak its name." But go back further and you'll find it *did* speak its name – sometimes quite loudly – in love letters, poetry, and art.

In short, the historical bedroom (or back alley, or palace chamber, or haystack – wherever) was not the monochrome, exclusively hetero place some imagine. Humans have always been adventurous and carnal creatures. They found ways to express their love and lust regardless of the taboos of later historians. So, myth busted: They definitely had real sex back then – and thanks to archaeologists and meticulous record-keepers, we have receipts.

Marriage (and bedroom) lesson: intimacy is a fundamental human experience. People will find ways to love each other physically, no matter the time or place. As the old saying goes, where there's a will, there's a way – and history shows there was plenty of will.

Myth Busted – "No Famous Historical Figures Were Gay"

Quick, name a famous LGBTQ person from history who isn't from the last century. Having a hard time? That's not because they didn't exist – it's because textbooks often politely ignored that part of their stories.

Let's fling open the closet doors of history and introduce a few star players who were batting for the other team (or both teams, or all teams – many swung every which way, fluidity isn't new either).

Alexander the Great – Yes, Mr. "I conquered the known world by age 30 and would have gone further if my army hadn't been tired" himself. Alexander was the king of Macedon in 4th century BCE and one of history's greatest military geniuses. And guess what? He had a male lover (or two, or three). His most famous romantic companion was Hephaestion, his childhood friend turned general, basically his ride-or-die soulmate. They grew up together under Aristotle's tutelage (imagine the study sessions…), fought side by side, and were so close that when they visited the tombs of Achilles and Patroclus (another famously tight ancient duo), Alexander laid a wreath on Achilles' tomb and Hephaestion on Patroclus' – symbolism much? When Hephaestion died suddenly, Alexander didn't just shed a tear; he lost it completely. He declared a period of national mourning, had doctors executed for failing to save his love (yikes, overkill), and possibly drank himself into a stupor. He even petitioned a god to grant Hephaestion divine honors. That's like naming a constellation after your boo, level 100 devotion. And Alexander wasn't alone – he also had a thing with a beautiful Persian youth named Bagoas. In one recorded episode, Alexander publicly kissed Bagoas after Bagoas won a dance contest. The Macedonian troops cheered wildly – apparently they shipped that relationship too. So anyone claiming no major historical leader was gay might need to, as Lizzo says, check their DNA – Alexander's legacy is literally bi (or pan) representation on a warhorse.

Emperor Hadrian – Jump to the Roman Empire, 2nd century CE. Hadrian is known for building that wall in Britain (to keep those pesky Scots out) and for being one of the "Five Good Emperors." But behind every good emperor is… maybe a really cute boyfriend. Hadrian's heart belonged to Antinous, a Greek youth of remarkable beauty. The two became inseparable, doing everything together – picture an imperial power tour with a plus-one in matching togas. Tragically, Antinous drowned in the Nile under mysterious circumstances when he was still in his late teens or early 20s. Hadrian was devastated. How did he cope? By basically turning Antinous into a god. He had countless statues made (you can still see Antinous' face in museums all over the world – the emperor's personal Insta feed in marble), founded an entire city in Egypt named Antinoopolis in his memory, and established a cult to worship him. People across the empire started venerating Antinous; he became a sort of unofficial saint of same-sex devotion. It's one of the most extravagant displays of love (and grief) by a leader in history. If that's not a famous gay love story, nothing is. Hadrian didn't publish sappy sonnets – he went and literally changed the religious landscape. (To put that in modern terms, it's like a billionaire tech mogul founding a new city and religion based on his beloved – wild, right?)

Queen Anne – Royal lady love alert! Anne ruled Great Britain in the early 1700s. She's less famous for her policies and more for the drama at her court which, thanks to a recent Oscar-winning film *The Favourite*, is now infamous. Anne had very intense relationships with two women in her life: Sarah Churchill (Duchess of Marlborough) and later Abigail Masham. Sarah was her confidante, advisor, and, if rumors and many historians are to be believed, the object of deep affection and possibly romantic love. They exchanged letters that read an awful lot like love letters – full of endearments and jealousy and pleas to not be "cast off." Sarah, being a strong-willed woman, sometimes bossed the Queen around (bold move, to say the least), and their spats could shake kingdoms (imagine a lovers' quarrel affecting parliamentary politics – that happened!). Eventually, Sarah was ousted and replaced in Anne's favor by Abigail, a quieter cousin of Sarah's who gave Anne the tenderness she craved without the attitude. The power triangle of Anne, Sarah, and Abigail was the talk of the town. Pamphleteers insinuated what was up (in pretty crude ways), and even then people *knew*. The whole situation was basically a high-stakes soap opera: *"Love, intrigue, and war – coming this fall, only on HBO: The Queen's Women."* Anne's story shows that yes, even a reigning queen might have had a love life that didn't fit the hetero fairy-tale mold. And she's far from the only one – there were several European queens and princesses with similar stories (Christina of Sweden dressed in men's clothes and likely romanced women; Catherine the Great wrote fondly to female friends, etc.). Royal courts were often hotbeds of not just political intrigue, but romantic variety.

James I of England (and VI of Scotland) – This guy united the crowns of Scotland and England in 1603 and is famous for commissioning the King James Bible translation. But King James had his own *chapters* of queer history. He had passionate favorites – male favorites – at court, the most notable being George Villiers, the Duke of Buckingham. James called Villiers things like "my sweetheart" and even "my wife" in letters. Yes, a king of England in the 17th century wrote to another man calling him his wife. Imagine the palace gossip! (The king also had a wife – Queen Anne of Denmark – but apparently he found room in his heart for both the Queen and the Duke, multitasking monarch that he was.) Detractors at the time murmured about the king's "ungodly" attachments, but James was powerful enough to basically ignore them. He knighted his lover, loaded him up with titles and riches, and kept him as close as possible. So, next time someone claims "no famous figure was gay," kindly remind them that an *actual King of England* was writing love letters to dudes.

Various U.S. and modern examples – It wasn't just the olden days in Europe and Asia. How about something closer to home and time? Many suspect that President Abraham Lincoln had an intimate relationship with his close friend Joshua Speed when they were young men sharing a bed (for four years, they lived together). Historians debate it fiercely – some saying "they were just very good friends, it was common to share beds back then!" and others winking "mmm hmmm, sure." We'll probably never know for sure, but the fact the question even arises tells you that sexuality is more diverse than the portraits in the history classroom. Or take Eleanor Roosevelt, beloved First Lady – she had a dear friend and likely lover named Lorena Hickok, with whom she exchanged reams of letters that make *The Notebook* look tame. Poets like Walt Whitman wrote odes about love between men ("We two boys together clinging" – subtle, Walt). The brilliant mathematician Alan Turing, as mentioned earlier, was not just the father of computing and AI but also an openly gay man (open to his friends, at least) at a time when it was a dangerous secret. Or creative geniuses like Michelangelo and Leonardo da Vinci – both had strong affections for men, evidenced by Michelangelo's sonnets and Leonardo's journal notes (and the fact both were lifelong bachelors who got in trouble with the law in their youth over trysts with male models). Oscar Wilde, the dazzling playwright, had a famous affair with Lord Alfred Douglas that landed him in jail. Gertrude Stein and Alice B. Toklas were an iconic lesbian couple hosting literary salons in 1920s Paris (Hemingway and Picasso dropped by their pad). And the list goes on: from emperors to artists, warriors to writers, LGBTQ folks have been among the ranks of the rich, powerful, and genius throughout history. The lack of a rainbow flag on their Wikipedia page doesn't mean it wasn't so – often it means past biographers brushed it under the rug.

To put it cheekily, history has always had a queer VIP section, even if it was sometimes hush-hush. The idea that no famous figures were gay is as laughable as saying no famous figures had red hair – it's just part of human variety, always has been. The difference is, until recently, you couldn't exactly list "Had a fabulous same-sex love life" as a line in the royal resume. But behind the scenes, it was there, shaping hearts and minds and sometimes even political events. Interpretive insight: Greatness and gayness (or any LGBTQ-ness) are not mutually exclusive – shocker! In fact, sometimes it seems like a little *queerness* was the secret sauce behind some historic achievements (or at least added to their intrigue). So let's give credit where credit is due and remember that our pantheon of heroes and luminaries has always been a bit more colorful than we were taught. It's history's echo indeed – we see ourselves in the past once we know where to look.

Marriage lesson: You can be legendary in your career *and* love who you love. Don't let anyone say your love holds you back – if Alexander and Hadrian and Anne and James could run empires and kingdoms with their beloved by their side, you can conquer whatever life throws at you with your special someone, thank you very much.

Myth Busted – "Society Has Always Been Anti-Gay"

Now for a myth that likes to masquerade as common sense: the claim that society, in all times and places, has been uniformly anti-gay until basically yesterday. According to this story, humanity was on one long, uninterrupted heterosexual picnic, rudely intruded upon by the modern LGBTQ movement. Time to debunk that with a hearty laugh and a history lesson: society's attitudes toward same-sex relationships have swung back and forth like a pendulum (or perhaps like Miley Cyrus on her wrecking ball – coming in hard one way, then the other).

In many ancient societies, same-sex love wasn't a huge deal. We've already seen how Greeks and Romans rolled. Ancient Greece basically gave homophobia a pass – at least for male relationships, and often for female ones too. While they didn't have Pride parades (tunics don't lend themselves to *twerking* on floats), they did have open acceptance in many city-states. Athens punished adulterers harshly but had no law against a man stepping out with another man. In Sparta, it was practically encouraged for young warriors to have a bond with an older warrior; they thought it made the army stronger. And then there's Thebes – a Greek city that took the idea "love is the strongest bond" very literally. They formed the Sacred Band of Thebes, an elite military unit composed of 150 male couples (yes, 300 men, each pair lovers). Why? Because they believed men who were in love would fight to the death to protect each other and also wouldn't dare show cowardice in front of their beloved. This gay military squad kicked butt across Greece for decades, until they heroically fell in battle against Philip of Macedon (Alexander the Great's dad). When Philip surveyed the bodies and learned who they were, he reportedly mourned their valor, saying "Perish any man who suspects that these men either did or suffered anything unseemly." In plain English: he was honoring how fierce and noble their love and loyalty made them. Not the reaction of a society that was *always* anti-gay, huh?

Moving eastward and forward in time, consider the medieval Islamic world. Surprise – many Islamic societies in the "Golden Age" (8th to 13th centuries) were quite laid-back about homosexuality, at least compared to the Christian Europe of the same time. Poets in Persia (modern-day Iran) wrote sultry ghazals about the beauty of young men with curls like hyacinths. Ottoman Turkey, even into the early modern era, was observed by European travelers to be relatively tolerant of male love – to the shock of those Europeans who had by then become quite prudish. An 18th-century French visitor might clutch his lace hanky upon seeing a Turkish vizier casually enjoying the company of a handsome boy, while the locals basically shrugged. It's not that these societies had rainbow flags flying, but homosexual conduct wasn't this huge criminalized taboo in many periods. It was more of a "don't ask, don't tell – but we all wink and know it happens" scenario.

In contrast, Europe went through a rough patch of intolerance, especially from the late Middle Ages onward. After Christianity became the dominant force, the Church's stance (influenced by certain interpretations of scripture) was that homosexual acts were a sin – the infamous "sin of Sodom." It took some time to ramp up, but by the medieval period, in many parts of Europe, being caught in a same-sex act could land you in serious trouble – shunned at best, executed at worst. (Medieval punishment for "sodomy" was sometimes death by fire. Let's just say the Middle Ages were not a great time for a gay barbecue – you might be the one on the grill.) However, even in this era, it wasn't uniformly enforced. Some areas looked the other way; some leaders had their favorites (hello, King James and others) and got away with it. And ironically, the Renaissance that followed brought a weird double standard: the art and literature celebrated homoerotic themes (Michelangelo painting those muscled Sistine Chapel nudes, Shakespeare writing sonnets to a "fair youth"), even as officially the laws stayed strict. It's like society couldn't make up its mind – praising the beauty of the male form with one hand, holding a morality club in the other.

Colonialism then spread these strict antisodomy laws around the globe like a bad cold. The British, for instance, left behind Section 377 (an anti-gay law) in almost every colony they ruled – India, Kenya, Jamaica, you name it, they got the Victorian anti-gay gift that kept on giving. A lot of places where homosexuality had been treated more casually suddenly had imported jail sentences for it. That's why you'll notice countries with a history of British rule often shared the same law code criminalizing gay sex (many have repealed it now, thankfully). It wasn't some home-grown perennial hatred; it was stamped in by a particular empire's moral code.

Then the pendulum started swinging back. By the late 19th and early 20th century, you had early movements in Europe campaigning (quietly) for tolerance – like Germany's Scientific-Humanitarian Committee in 1897 lobbying to decriminalize homosexuality. They didn't succeed then, but imagine even raising that in 1897 – bold! In the 1920s, Berlin was a hotspot of gay culture: lively clubs, drag balls, same-sex dances – society in that little bubble was, for a short golden moment, pretty accepting. It's no coincidence that the first known gender affirmation surgeries and openly trans individuals, as well as gay magazines, blossomed in Weimar Republic Germany. Society was experimenting with openness. Unfortunately, then came the Nazis, slamming the pendulum violently to the far right – they targeted LGBTQ people alongside Jews and others, sending them to concentration camps with pink triangle badges. Dark times indeed.

Post-WWII, many places were still rigid (1950s America, for instance, was not exactly Pride-friendly; they were busy witch-hunting gay people out of government jobs in the "Lavender Scare"). But then the groundwork for change had been laid. The swinging sixties (and Stonewall in '69, back to where we started this chapter) sent the pendulum careening towards freedom again. Since then, despite some backlash here and there, the overall trajectory has been towards more acceptance, not less. Countries began decriminalizing (the UK in 1967 for example, albeit partially; the US via court decisions by 2003; India striking down that colonial law in 2018 – a huge reversal of a supposedly "always this way" law). And beyond decriminalization, social attitudes have thawed dramatically in many parts of the world. What was scandalous is now just a shrug or a celebratory cheer.

To be fair, not every society is on the same page yet. Some places are unfortunately still stuck in a homophobic hangover, enforcing harsh penalties and intolerance (we see you, and we hope the rainbow reaches you soon). But the myth we're busting is the *"always"* part – as if humanity unanimously hated the idea of two men or two women in love from day one. That's just not true. There have been highs and lows, bright spots and dark ages. The ancient world had plenty of open-minded moments. The early modern non-Western world too. It's really the last several hundred years where a particular strain of puritanical, colonial, and religious fervor made it pretty bad in many places. And now, in a twist of fate, modern times are looking more like the tolerant ancient times (in some ways even more tolerant, since now we talk openly about rights and celebrate queer identity). It's like we rediscovered a part of our humanity that was there all along but got buried under some dogma.

In summary, society hasn't "always" been anti-gay – society has been variable, evolving, sometimes surprisingly chill with it, sometimes horribly oppressive. But the good news is, the long arc, especially now, is bending toward inclusion. Cultures that once persecuted are apologizing (the UK literally "pardoned" Alan Turing and thousands of others posthumously – a symbolic but meaningful act). Pride celebrations are global. It's not uniform – we can't kid ourselves; there's work to do – but neither was the past uniformly hostile. Many ancestors would be baffled by the idea that love needed an "okay." Some might even say, "We celebrated it back in my day, welcome to the party!" History's echo: we're echoing the open attitudes of many an era gone by, but with the new twist of enshrining equality in law and culture.

So the next time someone shrugs and says "well, society has always been against this," you can reply with a confident grin: "Actually, not really. It's more like a pendulum, and right now it's swinging fabulously in favor of love." And if they protest, just remind them that even ancient warriors had boyfriends and entire temples were carved with same-sex lovers – if that isn't a loud echo from history supporting the cause, I don't know what is. Marriage lesson: Societal attitudes change, sometimes for worse, often for better. Don't let anyone tell you acceptance is a fluke. If anything, acceptance is a return to an age-old normalcy – loving our neighbors and letting them love who they love. In the grand scheme, prejudice is the historical blip, not love. Love, as we've seen, is the echo that never dies out.

(And they lived happily ever after – with pride.)

Epilogue

From ancient Egyptian tombs where two male lovers lie nose-to-nose to modern couples holding hands at Starbucks, history has a clear message: same-sex love has always been here. Indeed, the past has sported a rainbow-tinted footnote, even if chroniclers sometimes wrote it in invisible ink.

Throughout the ages, resilient queer love found ways to bloom in unlikely places. When society frowned, lovers got creative – passing coded letters, posing as "roommates" or "best friends," often living on the fringes – but live they did, vibrantly so. Even Oscar Wilde's imprisonment for "gross indecency" backfired – his ordeal sparked outrage that fueled change. Every whispered endearment and clandestine waltz was a small act of revolution, gradually chipping away at the walls of prejudice.

Fast-forward to 1969: one summer night, patrons of the Stonewall Inn said "enough" – and ignited a movement. That spark lit a fire under decades of activism. Now each June, Pride parades march to commemorate that rebellion. Legal victories followed in courtrooms and parliaments, and the dominoes of progress continue to fall. In 2015, love won loud and clear when the United States legalized same-sex marriage nationwide. By 2025, 38 countries had done the same – and the list keeps growing.

Pop culture, too, has joined the party. These days superheroes come out and kids' cartoons casually feature two moms or two dads. From the silver screen to streaming, same-sex love stories are winning hearts. Imagine telling a 16th-century poet that an animated aardvark's teacher would have a same-sex wedding on TV – absurdly magical, but true! The world now dances to songs by queer artists, and even corporate logos can't resist a rainbow makeover each June. The love that once *dared not speak its name* now belts showtunes at top volume in the town square.

As we close this rollicking, truth-telling adventure, the final pages flutter with hope. The resilience and vibrancy of same-sex couples is legendary – and it lights the way forward. We honor the struggles and triumphs of those who came before. Their legacy lives on every time a child reads a fairy tale with a same-sex royal wedding and thinks it's perfectly normal. The journey isn't over, but what a joy it is to see how far we've come. May future generations look back on our time and say, "They lived, they loved, they persisted – and isn't that fabulous?"

www.ingramcontent.com/pod-product-compliance
Lightning Source LLC
Chambersburg PA
CBHW061752120626
46550CB00005B/1970